FLICKERS OF MERCY
IN THE SONORAN DESERT OF ARIZONA

By

Monsignor Michael Otto Ekpenyong

Cover design by Monsignor Michael Otto Ekpenyong
Front cover photograph by George J. Dowling
Back cover photograph by Steve Davis

ISBN 978-1-940985-38-1

Printed in the United States of America
First Printing: July 2016

Table of Contents

Dedication

To our twin siblings:
Their twin meteoric lives and twin deaths
incarnated in our mother Margaret,
"The Anthem of Mercy."

Itoro eti Eka – A Mother's Praise

Afo okoboho mkpa ini manade;

Okodu uwem ini uman okurede;

Kpukpru enyong ye kpukpru isong;

Etoro fi uyai uwem ukpong!

You escaped death when I was born;

You lived when the birth pains were over;

All the heavens and all the earth;

Praise your beauty of Soul!

Thanksgiving for God's Everlasting Mercy
(Psalm 136: 1-9, 23-26)

Praise the Lord for he is good;
For his mercy endures forever;
Praise the God of gods;
For his mercy endures forever;
Praise the Lord of lords;
For his mercy endures forever;
Who alone does wonders,
For his mercy endures forever;
Who skillfully made the heavens,
For his mercy endures forever;
Who spread the earth upon the waters,
For his mercy endures forever;
Who made the great lights,
For his mercy endures forever;
The sun to rule the day,
For his mercy endures forever;
The moon and the stars to rule the night,
For his mercy endures forever.
The Lord remembered us in our low estate,
For his mercy endures forever;
Freed us from our foes,
For his mercy endures forever;
And gives bread to all flesh,
For his mercy endures forever.
Praise the God of heaven,
For his mercy endures forever.

Introduction

I present the story of St. Joseph as an entry story into this book of reflections, <u>Flickers of Mercy</u>. What challenges us is the person of St. Joseph. Who was he and who is he for us? He says nothing and nobody hears him say anything. Instead, he is told what to do and he listens and does what he is told to do. He plays one of the loudest roles in the history of our salvation but he is simply an enigma. He is called husband of Mary by both the writers of the gospels and an angelic being, but the child that comes from the union of Joseph and Mary is without the biological contribution of Joseph as the husband.

And the question becomes an extended quest for a seemingly elusive personality. How does one get around to knowing the silent and enigmatic Joseph? Our starting point is the narrative in Scripture about Joseph by St. Matthew.

The angel in a dream revealed to Joseph that the child Mary was carrying was the Son of God, *"For it is through the Holy Spirit that this child has been conceived in her"* (Mt. 1:20). There is no record of Joseph's emotional reaction anywhere in the gospels. But there is the record of him doing what the angel told him to do. *"When Joseph awoke, he did as the angel of the Lord had commanded him and took his wife into his home"* (Mt. 1:24). And the sacred writer notes the fact that, *"He had no relations with her until she bore a son, and he named him Jesus"* (Mt. 1:25).

There are two issues here to be clarified about the Jewish marriage culture in Joseph's time to help bring to human reason the type of relationship that existed between Joseph and Mary. The Jewish marriage culture involved two steps, namely, betrothal and marriage proper[1]. Betrothal was the formal exchange of consent before witnesses. It took place when the bride was 12 or 13 years old and the suggested age for the bridegroom was 18. After the betrothal, the bride legally belonged to the bridegroom, but she remained with her parents until the public marriage commitment and the joyful celebration that followed. During this period, the marriage could only be broken by a legal divorce.

From the evidence of the gospel, the betrothal of Mary to Joseph had taken place: *"Now this is how the birth of Jesus came about: When his mother Mary was betrothed to Joseph, but before they lived together…"* (Mt. 1:18). Joseph was yet to take Mary, his legal bride, to his family home. It was at this point that the divine intervention erupted.

The second issue is about the options that were open to Joseph in the circumstances of Mary's pregnancy. By strict Jewish law, Joseph could have allowed the law to take its course by going ahead with the divorce process of presenting a written evidence of official divorce from Mary signed by two witnesses[2]. With this, Mary would become a kind of "persona non grata," a shameless object fit only for ridicule, and she would have been left to pay the penalty of breaking the bond of marriage. In practical terms, she would be game for stoning to death by the people of the village.

Joseph thought about the whole issue but decided to act differently. He was no dummy. He knew the marriage laws of his people well but decided to become the prosecutor, the defense, the judge and the only jury in his case. He would apply the law "mercifully" by divorcing Mary quietly. The adverb "mercifully" is used with a semantic intent. It gives us a clue to the meaning and the personality of Joseph. The word mercy in Latin is 'Misericordia.' It is a compound word that bridges *'miseria'*, meaning 'misery' and *'cor'*, meaning 'heart'.

Misericordia literally means *'heart overwhelmed by misery.'* In this narrative, we can imagine with what Mary was burdened. Humanly speaking, both psychologically and socially, Mary was a mental and physical wreck and ruin, only good for public sport and scorn. She had divine support[3], but how would she break the news? How could she honestly look at Joseph to tell her story? Would she dare to face Joseph face to face, eye to eye? What words would describe the apparent betrayal? In every respect, misery drowned her out. With Joseph, nothing was simple either. But there seemed to have been a catalyst in process. Joseph put himself in the being and place of Mary. In himself, he felt and relived the *'misery'* of Mary.

There is no doubt that Joseph, as a human being, was shocked to have realized that Mary was pregnant and he knew he was not responsible for it. Should we describe Joseph's attitude as pity, sympathy, anger, confusion, or sincere empathy? More than these very core human feelings, Joseph loved Mary. His heart bled and reflected the misery that, like waves, were pounding Mary's heart. With star-light courage, he chose his "never-yet-travelled" path of Misericordia. In him, misery found a compassionate heart.

Can we at this point answer the lead question of who Joseph was? It would seem that Joseph was a man gifted like all of us with a plethora of virtues. But he cultivated their seeds – gentleness, patience, humility, kind-heartedness, courage and magnanimity in his depths. He did this in preparation for his task as foster father of the divine child who was placed in his trust. From him and under his tutelage, Jesus would grow, learn and experience raw mercy from birth. His hidden years were years walking and working in the light of a household of mercy.

From the carpenter's workshop to the temple and the synagogue, Jesus was served and immersed in an enabling environment of mercy. He must have had Joseph in eternal remembrance when, later in the paradigmatic Sermon on the Mount, he said, *"Blessed are the merciful, for they shall obtain mercy"* (Mt. 5:7). And out on the roads of Palestine on his evangelizing mission, in his symbolic and metaphoric stories, mercy would become the staple healing *Haggadah*[4] for human spirits for ages unending. Like Joseph, Jesus choose to cultivate a spiritual path, as was the case in going into the desert to search for wisdom and inner strength (Lk. 4:1-13) and also going up the Mount of Transfiguration to pray (Luke 9:28-36).

With Joseph in the carpenter's workplace, Jesus learned the meaning of *"Never say never until never transforms into Eureka (my personal motto),"* meaning that perseverance is key in life. That experience would inspire him to create the "Parable of the Fig Tree" (Lk. 13:1-9). From the unconventional love story of his parents, Mary and Joseph, he came to understand the meaning of prodigal loving, which gave him insight to tell the "Parable of the Prodigal Son" (Lk. 151-3, 11-32). From Mary or Joseph, Jesus must have learned about the big-heartedness of Joseph, choosing the path of mercy rather than judgment in the difficult circumstances of Mary's pregnancy. That story of Joseph's magnanimity stirred up in Jesus' fertile imagination the "Parable of the woman caught in adultery" (Jn. 8:1-11). In human living and relationships, appearances lead to false judgements more often than not. In life, things may not always fit into human standards of "black and white, right and wrong." So Jesus posed the challenge, *"Let the one without sin throw the first stone"* (Jn. 8:7).

If you are wondering about what I am up to, it is nothing other than imagining the origins of the seeds of Jesus' stories, parables and metaphors on mercy. On the human level I simply credit Joseph and Mary for giving their son good formation in their Jewish worldview that enhanced his ministry of Mercy. From them he learned the true meaning of mercy – love that is not self-regarding but goes beyond justice and the self. What are parents and guardians for, if not to be merciful guides and mentors? For Jesus, Joseph was a great example of mercy. And we are all beneficiaries. To his other titles we now can add "Joseph, Patron Saint of Mercy!" Here we can understand why St. Matthew prefaced his gospel with a careful narrative seen from Joseph's perspective. Joseph was for him a model of mercy. He planned to tell Joseph's story of mercy first in anticipation of his own tale of mercy later in his gospel. He was one of those that the Pharisees identified as "tax collectors and sinners," people hated by all. But the Lord Jesus, son of Mary and Joseph, saw him through the eyes of mercy and offered him eternal salvation (Mt. 9:9-13).

For Matthew, who sees God and his relationship with us from St. Joseph's world view, mercy is a cardinal virtue for human happiness yet to be fully understood and cultivated. Now we can understand why Pope Francis, like Matthew, saw his apostolic ministry through the eyes of St. Joseph, for mercy is the music of the soul and of the universe. The words on his Coat of Arms, *"Miserando Atque Eligendo"* is the Latin for *"To be shown mercy and chosen"*. Pope Francis has embraced Joseph's *"Misericordia"* in order to identify his call to the papal ministry with the call of Matthew to tell the story of God's mercy, for life would be a lot less complicated with a little bit of mercy from everyone for everyone. And all this because Joseph knew God, believed God, trusted God and played his part.

From the above reflection on the texts of the Gospel we can reasonably answer the question: "Who was Joseph?" He was not only a merciful man but he was also a model of Mercy! What does Joseph mean for us as we read and reflect on the texts and thoughts contained in Flickers of Mercy? A lot to ponder that can help us refigure, configure and become better beings of mercy. I wonder about the imagination of Joseph at that defining moment of salvation history. He cultivated his imaginative garden of mercy in space and time and left us the seeds of mercy to sow for our difficult times.

We might do well to imagine more and open new paths for human kind to be gentler and kinder to each other. I reflect on the look, the touch, the embrace and the other ways of human relating between Joseph and Mary that greatly impacted Jesus. In Jesus, and through Jesus, there are perspectives of mercy yet for us, to use to help us build a better world. In such a world, mercy givers will know the true meaning of being there for others and mercy receivers will ever be thankful to God, the source of mercy. I contemplate the listening of Joseph to Mary at the saddest moment of human bonding, and I believe our decisions will be life-giving when we listen to each other with sympathy, empathy and above all with prodigal love.

The reflections in the pages of <u>Flickers of Mercy</u> symbolize – flickers, moments, and possibilities of how to be human in order to replenish the deficit of Mercy in our century. Mercy is God who is I Am. As partakers of God's being, mercy is our very being. It does take effort to fan it into contagious flames. I need to be infected by the sparks of other missionaries' contagion and together we can turn the world of our day upside down by giving into the heart of misery as did Joseph and Mary and Jesus. Let us work as if all the world depends on us for mercy and pray because mercy is God's gift.

Pope Francis inaugurated and set a limit to the Jubilee Year of Mercy (December 8, 2015 – November 20, 2016). But he didn't mean that mercy is human work for one year only. He was rather calling us to consciously revisit a cardinal virtue and to make it a habit in our lives. I, therefore, believe that the Jubilee Year is a beginning; and it is a call to all of us to join the

Pope to work to make mercy the culture for all generations. In this sense Flickers of Mercy looks at the bigger picture of mercy ahead; and it humbly exhorts all of us to become co-workers of mercy with the Pastor of Mercy, Pope Francis. The Noble Prize Poet Laureate, Rudyard Kipling once said, *"If history were taught in the form of stories, it would never be forgotten"*[5]. I have embraced the insight of Kipling by crafting lived human experiences into the narratives of Flickers of Mercy to prolong in time and eternity our divine-human conversation.

As you read these narratives of Flickers of Mercy, be sure to recollect your moments of mercy too, to benefit others in the unending circle of: *Mercy-telling* and *Mercy-retelling*, *Mercy-listening* and *Mercy-remembering*, *Mercy-reading* and *Mercy becoming*. That is how God did it from the beginning. He created us in Mercy. He told us stories of the merciful people he created. You are one of them. I have adopted the Socratic method of raising questions in some chapters to challenge us to embrace radical mercy; in others I have concluded with prayers trusting in God's faithfulness and the guidance of the Holy Spirit.

Prayer to St. Joseph:

Saint Joseph, illustrious descendant of David,

Husband of the Mother of God,

Foster father of the Son of God,

In a dream you received from the Almighty

The task of taking Mary as your wife

And Jesus as your son, conceived from the Holy Spirit,

And of caring for them in the difficult beginnings of the New Covenant.

Intercede for us so that your example may remind us to care for the presence of Jesus and Mary in our lives, in the trials of today's world.

-     *From Blessings and Prayers for Home and Family*

1. Abraham Cohen, Everyman's Talmud, Birmingham, December 1931. www.bnpublishing.com, pp. 171-179.

2. Ibid. p. 177.

3. *Haggadah* is a legend or parable to illustrate a point of law in the Talmud.

4. Gospel of St. Luke 1:26-38.

5. AZQuotes.com website: //www.azquotes.com/author/8083-Rudyard_Kipling.

Forward

All around the world, the Roman Catholic Church is celebrating a Year of Mercy in which Pope Francis has exhorted us to encounter a God of boundless mercy and compassion. In Flickers of Mercy, Msgr. Michael Ekpenyong provides us with mercy moments from his own rich experience both at home in Nigeria, in other African nations as well as his recent service at St. Pius X Parish, in the Sonoran Desert, in the Diocese of Tucson.

He introduces the reader to the Rwandan notion of "Gachacha", similar to our notion of restorative justice, in which the offender and the offended move toward understanding and forgiveness. His stories and use of Scripture throughout the text, powerfully bring home the notion of mercy in concrete and vivid ways.

Building a world of peace is a passion of Msgr. Michael and he calls us to be "missionaries of mercy", who work to soothe differences and to resolve conflicts that separate and divide people in our families and communities.

This pastoral text brings mercy alive through the reflections of a true pastor who seeks to lead his people closer to Jesus Christ who is the font of mercy. The text leads us in the Year of Mercy, not only to celebrate but to live mercy as a key attribute of God and what should characterize those who want to be disciples of this loving God.

You will enjoy, as I did, learning about the various facets of mercy described in the book and how we might make mercy come alive in our lives.

The chapters include reflections Msgr. Ekpenyong shared with his people at St. Pius X Parish and so can be beneficial to any pastor who wants to help his people understand better the notion of mercy, which is characteristic of God throughout the Scriptures and the focus for this Year of Mercy

Most Rev. Gerald F. Kicanas, D.D., Bishop of the Catholic Diocese of Tucson, Arizona

Acknowledgements

One morning after our liturgical celebration, Linda and David Mount, Sister Theresa Martin, CSI, and Sister Barbara Donahue, CSJ, stopped me by the Church entrance and said with cordial but proactive exhortation: "It would be good if you could keep record of your reflections and maybe make it available to us and others." I do not remember my immediate response to this insightful quartet but I gave a thought to their exhortation. Flickers of Mercy owes much to their encouraging and kind words. To these disciples of wisdom and mercy, I can say: Fellow missionaries of mercy, your exhortation triggered in my theological imagination, the need to birth and feed the people of God and take pastoral responsibility in the Jubilee Year of Mercy. Thank you my Brother and Sisters in Christ.

The pastorally-focused Pastor, Father Harry Ledwith, and the staff of St. Pius X, have made this book of reflections possible by letting me experience concretely the reality and the meaning of mercy. Their incredible commitment to service makes St. Pius X Parish, a living model school of Mercy. The Pastoral unit, under the diligent watch of Karen Horton, made available to me the necessary lectionary resource materials that assisted my reflections. Kudos to you the star-light mercy team of St. Pius X: Deacon Denis Ranke, Barbara Dowling, Teri Olaje, Aggy Froehlke, Deanne Lialios, Linda Alexander, Kim Timmermann, Abraham Marcor, David Bellamy, Rachel Brena, Paul Flores, Pat Brena, Tina Cohen and Lena Englert. Thank you dear colleagues in the service of Mercy.

From the administrative witness to mercy, the parishioners have caught "the mercy bug" in their passion and compassionate deeds for Mercy. I thank Joan and John Kaltsas and Joanne Adams who read through the texts of our book and made insightful remarks for further meaningful reflections. The pages of <u>Flickers of Mercy</u> do not pretend to take for granted the St. Pius X enabling environment from which the seeds of Mercy were sown. The motto of St. Pius X: *"To renew all things in Christ"* has been vividly lived, creatively explored and is still ongoing. I pray that <u>Flickers of Mercy</u> will encourage all parishioners on our Lord's mission of Mercy for our times, *"Blessed are the merciful for they will be shown mercy"* (Mt. 5:7).

Bishop Gerald F. Kicanas deserves a paragraph all his own. Knowing the nature of the heavy schedule of the Chief Pastor of the Diocese during Holy Week, I had the temerity to ask him to write the foreword for <u>Flickers of Mercy</u>. The thought of seeing him for this purpose did not come easy but I thought I should try. He did not disappoint me at all. "When do you want it?" he asked with a smile. Listen to me say with tongue in cheek, "After Easter, My Lord!" And exactly one week after Easter, Bishop Kicanas submitted his foreword to me. Come to think of what I did: I made an appointment to see the Bishop and I also decided when I wanted his gift of a foreword! Do you understand the lesson that Bishop Kicanas has taught me? His attitude is itself a lesson about flickers of mercy – words empowered with action. *"Je vous remercie, mon Eveque Gerald F. Kicanas!"*

To the many, within and outside St. Pius X faith community, who have reached out to me by a smile, a laugh, a hug, a word, a thought, a prayer, a card or a note, I express deep appreciation. With Flickers of Mercy, let us together celebrate the festival of Mercy for our century.

In writing these reflections, I have used "The Saint Joseph's Edition of The New American Bible, Revised Edition" as my main biblical reference document. The Sunday lectionary of Year C within the Jubilee Year of Mercy has provided me with contextual readings that guided the reflections. "Workbook for Lectors, Gospel Readers, and Proclaimers of Word, 2016, United States Edition," with its storied and learned commentaries, was used as a kind of Lectio Divina for prayerful refection. Reading through the 2015 monthly issues of "Celebration, A Comprehensive Worship Resource," especially, it's "Sermon Starters" encouraged me to weave lived human experiences into the narratives of Flickers of Mercy.

As a theological method, lived human experiences told as stories can serve as daily practical theology, a medium by which the good news about God-human relationship is narrated in a manner that people can more easily open up to, understand and embrace for their life's journey. The 2014/2015/2016 issues of "Pastoral Patterns," World Library Publications, with its typical "Questions for the Day," method gave me insight into questioning as a tool for daily incarnational practical theology, challenging people to self-examination for lives well-lived as Christ's authentic disciples.

The traditional saying of my people holds that: *"Ifiok edi etibe"*, meaning that "Knowledge is contribution". With deep gratitude, I have benefitted from the ideas of many but I take full responsibility for the mistakes in <u>Flickers of Mercy</u>

Chapter One. A Historic Moment to Mercy

On December 8, 2015, in Rome, Pope Francis marked "A Historic Moment to Mercy" by opening the Door of Mercy to inaugurate the Jubilee Year of Mercy. He used that occasion to invite Christians and all people of good will to reflect, contemplate and practically witness to the mystery of God's Mercy in our world. In this opening chapter, we reflect on the challenge to open the doors of our hearts to God's merciful love for us and to become bearers of God's merciful love to others, despite our inadequacies. For this purpose, I will use a secular text and the following scriptural texts: Isaiah 6:1-8; 1 Corinthians 15:1-11 and Luke 5:1-11.

In the ancient document the "Desiderata"[6], the unknown author commands his audience to be committed to the source of their well-being in order to enjoy life in its fullness: *"You are a child of the universe no less than the trees and the stars. You have a right to be here. ... Be at peace with God. ... Keep peace in your soul."* The Prophet Isaiah, St. Paul, and St. Peter, together with the first disciples and us, need to listen to and embrace the wise command of the ancient sage. We must freely, passionately and truthfully accept our mission on behalf of God-in-Christ.

The stories told, in the Sacred Scriptures, of the attitude of the friends of God who are called to mission, seem to reflect an ignorance of the full story of who we are as sons and daughters of God. Their words reflect their attitudes of fear or inadequacy. *"Woe is me, a man of unclean lips…"* (Is 6:5), says Prophet Isaiah. *"For I am the least of the Apostles, not fit to be called an apostle…"* (1Cor 15:9), says St. Paul, *"Depart from me, for I am a sinner"* (Lk 5:8), says St. Peter.

We may know people, in our families and communities, who consider themselves useless and not fit for God's purposes. Thus we can relate to Prophet Isaiah, St. Paul and St. Peter in their self-perception as not good enough for the task. When we think, believe, and proclaim that we are useless or afraid, our mediocrity will breathe out mediocrity to others. But God proclaims, in style our magnificence in Him,

2

calling us by name and owning us even before we were born (Jer. 1:5; Is. 43:1, 7; 49:15-16).

When we think we are inadequate, we tend to act without self-confidence and trust in God. Timidity robs us of the enabling power of the Good News that in God we have enough to enjoy life in all its fullness. The abundance of what we are in God gives us the courage to say that we are magnificent, and special; yes, I am! Yes, you are! Aren't we? Knowing this truth of our being in God prepares us for a fruitful mission to rescue fellow sojourners in mediocrity, from mediocrity, into a fullness of life where we can bear fruit in plenty of starlight for Mercy.

In the Jubilee Year of Mercy, the Universal Mother Church calls us to be "missionaries of mercy." *"Nemo dat quod non habet –You cannot give what you do not have"* is the saying of sages for ages. We can only give of what we have in God as revealed in Christ. We are called to acknowledge and share with all the compassion of God beyond world views, borders, rules, color, gender and creed. We are called to return to mercy and be on a mission of mercy. With St. Paul, we must *"hand on"* to all, all of who we are and all we have received, God's ever gentle, passionate compassion and merciful love revealed in Christ. Never blush nor fret then for I call you magnificent daughters and sons, for that is what you are in God-in-Christ. Magnificent daughters and sons of God, will you consider becoming "missionaries of mercy?"

Who do you know in your village, town or city or beyond your village, town or city that might be longing for God's unconditional compassionate and merciful care? Should you worry, as Isaiah did of his unworthiness, be assured, the Lord of hosts has *"touched you, your wickedness is removed, your sin is purged"* (Is 6:7). Should you feel guilty as St. Paul did, be assured, by the grace of God you are what you are and God's grace is with you and is enough for you on your mission (1Cor 15:10). Should you be afraid as St Peter was, then be assured of the Lord's power to transform a timid fisherman into a Rocky rescuer of people into well-being (Lk 5:1-11). Are you ready to be journeying on your healing mission of mercy? You have heard the voice of the Lord saying, *"Whom shall I send? Who will go for us?"* *"Here am I!"* *Dare to say: "Send me!"* (Is 6:8).

> *Lord God,*
> *by your Grace*
> *we are what we are,*
> *magnificent beings of your gifted grace.*
> *May your gracious gifts in us be in*
> *abundance*
> *to power our local and global works of*
> *mercy!*
> *May we at this historic moment of grace*
> *open our hearts to "Mercy Incarnate",*
> *to win us your peace and keep peace in*
> *our souls!*
> *Amen.*

6. Treasurable philosophy found in a 12th Century Cathedral, author unknown.

Chapter Two. The Anthem of Mercy

In this chapter the gospel story of the leper in Mark 1:40-45 will help us reflect on the experience of all forms of alienation in our midst. The experience of being restored creates an attitude of thankfulness so joyous that it deserves a never ending song. I call it "The Anthem of Mercy" because, in the Jubilee year of Mercy, the attitude of thankfulness is what all should ask God to renew in us. I will use a personal family story to get us started.

My mother, Margaret, became a twin-mother in the early 1950s. In the local culture, twins were considered symbols of evil. Thus, when Margaret became a twin-mother, she became an outcast, barred from her home, communal public domains, friends, and the village people. Even after the death of the twins, within a few days, in grief, she withdrew into herself. As a five- year-old-child, at that time, I couldn't understand how the joy and spontaneity that once identified our mother disappeared.

But now, as an adult, I have grown in the knowledge of my peoples' local culture. I now understand more of the evil that destroyed my mother's joy and human dignity. I have also learned much from my mother's experiences of being alienated. For years, each time I visited with her in the village, I would ask her to tell me her "twin-mother story." She would say nothing to me; she could not find words adequate enough to pour out her long bottled-up traumas. Finally, one day she was able to find the words, and she did so with tears. At the end she pleaded with me "to forgive the past".

I recall here, in my own words, what she told me that evening after dinner about her life as "a mother who bore two children at the same time." With no place to safely call home, she and our father moved from place to place seeking shelter. In the process she became an object of scorn for some and pity for others. As one who was usually the first to wake up in the morning and go to the stream with her black ebony pot, she could no longer do so. She was considered a bearer of evil omens to be avoided. With her remaining four children taking refuge at the homes of extended family members, she lost the joy that all mothers' share -- to care for and watch their little ones grow up.

With no twin-children to whom to sing her soothing "lullabies"anymore, she would often sing, about herself to herself, the traditional dirge: "*Owo nkpo nam – a person of sorrow*." As she told her story, she broke down in tears and pain. And there was I watching my mother weeping! *Yes, Margaret, at your command, I have forgiven the past. But I cannot forget the pains you have carried, in your heart alone, all these years about us your children. Accept our eternal gratitude, our merciful mother.*

As one can imagine, the wounds to Margaret's motherhood took time to heal. The healing began when she turned totally to the Church. The Word of God was the biggest source of her healing. Her total immersion in the Church's sacramental structures and pious groups helped her find meaning again in life. Becoming a "born again" Christian, Margaret found inner peace in a new home, where she made new friends, and found a new voice in the gospel of Jesus Christ.

Margaret's "dis-ease" was not leprosy. But, like the leper man in the gospel, she shared the same social "dis-ease" of exclusion and its attendant physical, psychological, and spiritual pains (Mk. 1:40-45). At the fringes of society, people become objects of dehumanizing pity rather than subjects of humanizing gladness and joyful presence. With exclusion from communal rituals, victims feel separated even from God. This is where the reaction of the leper, in the gospel, in the presence of Jesus, strikes a universal common human chord: *"If you wish,"* said the leper to Jesus, *"you can make me clean"* (Mk. 1:40).

Margaret would understand the leper's feelings, for both wanted Jesus to liberate and restore them into the community of loving sons and daughters of God. Jesus' response is tellingly unique in making the point that as human beings created in the image and likeness of God, they were never alienated in the first place. They were and are and will be beloved of God, for in God's house human dignity, freedom, equality, justice, compassion, mercy, forgiveness, empathy, and solidarity reign: *"I do will it. Be made clean!"* (Mk. 1:41).

The reactions of the healed leper man and the restored Margaret ignore Jesus' strong command not to tell people about their liberator. With their new-found freedom they, and all of us, simply must tell of their blessings about:

1. Life, children, immediate and extended families and friends;
2. The times and places of life in their world, with the moments of singing and dancing and weeping;
3. The births of every new human being as unique creations of the Creator;
4. The nurturance of their caretakers, parents, foster parents and guardians;
5. God's loving mercies in restoring our human rights, dignities, and being included in communities of love and compassion with our divine destiny in heaven; and
6. Those times when forgiveness of our deeply rooted inadequacies offered reconciliation with Christ Jesus.

For all these and more, our gratitude is boundless. Even when Jesus cautions us from going public, we cannot but keep singing of our gratitude. That is what Mercy makes us "be-come": people of the *"Be-attitudes," figured, re-configured, and transfigured into "divine mercy-hood."*

In the Jubilee Year of Mercy, gratitude is our anthem. With St. Paul, we *"Rejoice always! Pray constantly! In all circumstances, [we] give thanks, for that is the Will of God for [us] in Christ Jesus" (1Thess. 5:16-18).*

*Lord Jesus,
bless all mothers.
Keep us mindful and grateful for their
self-sacrifices. As we forgive all forms of
alienation of the past and the present, in
gratitude, make us agents of
enlightenment on the dignity of the
human person. By our merciful deeds
may we never repeat the past!
"Redeem us because of your mercy!"
(Psalm 44:27b)
Amen.*

Chapter Three. The Terms of Mercy

What model of justice serves for healing relations between peoples in the violent ridden towns, cities and nations of our world? Sometimes no model is good enough to address concrete cases in all places. In such situations we are challenged to become creative as was the case 22 years ago in the East African country of Rwanda. In "The Terms of Mercy" I will use the scriptural texts of Ezekiel 37:12-14; Romans 8:8-11 and John 11:1-45 to reflect on the ongoing concrete healing of human relations in Rwanda.

Years after the 1994 genocide in Rwanda, the people are still trying to come to terms with the truth of forgiveness as the condition for peace. A "Truth Commission" is the means by which forgiveness is being fostered in that once almost 95% Catholic Christian country. At a Peacebuilding Workshop in Kigali in 2005, a team of concerned local leaders and university teachers made classroom presentations on the local approach to truth and forgiveness called *"Gachacha"*. It involves the offender and the offended parties being brought by the community to dialogue with each other. The offender openly acknowledges his/her misdeed against the offended, and the offended freely accepts or rejects the regrets of the offender. At that point both parties are either reconciled or the community, depending on the complexity of the offense, decides on other terms to ensure justice and truth. After the simulated classroom presentations the participants were taken to an actual situation in a rural parish where the *"Gachacha"* truth and forgiveness process was taking place.

The setting was a lunch time meal. In a corner of the dining room were a young man in his early twenties and an adult man in his sixties, but who looked as though he was in his late eighties. They were eating together. The narrative following their table-fellowship was that the young man had personally and before the community confessed that he was the one who led the group that killed the wife and children of the elderly man. Addressing the visiting "Peace building team", the young man repeated his misdeeds. The elderly man, for all intents and purposes, was "dead-bones-sitting". When asked about his feelings towards the young man, the man hesitated momentarily in order to gather his finer human thoughts. Then, with eyes overwhelmed with tears and with shaking hands to cover his doubly wrinkled face, he shook his head before saying in the local dialect, "Now alone, I have him as my family!"

For him, what kept him alive was both hearing the truth of what happened to his wife and children and then offering forgiveness and mercy to their killer/s, such as his faith had taught him. His gift to his wife and children was to live on in the life-giving freedom that his act of mercy then gave him. He believed in life after life; and that he will meet again with his loved ones in the resurrection of the dead at the end of time.

The *"Gachacha"* narrative of Rwanda brings us to a deeper appreciation of God's power to raise us from our "dead bones." The challenge is to always walk the journey in the new life that merciful – forgiveness brings us. The "dead-bones-sitting" of Rwanda compares to Prophet Ezekiel's famous *"dead bones"* (Ezekiel 37:12-14). We can contemplate God's Spirit breathing life into them. With St. Paul, we can understand the living hope that kept the "dead-bones-sitting" alive. He lived in the Spirit-given life of the Risen Christ (Rom. 8:8-11). Like Martha in John's gospel, he believed in the future resurrection of his family members (Jn. 11:1-45). Jesus proclaims, *"I am the resurrection and the life; whoever believes in me, even if he dies, will live, and everyone who lives and believes in me will never die."*

Like the disciples of Jesus and like us, the "dead-bones-sitting" of Rwanda believed that eternal life is not life procrastinated but life lived even now. *"This is Eternal life, that they should know you, the only true God, and the one you sent, Jesus Christ"* (Jn. 17:3). We can appreciate why the "dead-bones-sitting" of Rwanda was weeping and shaking because we appreciate why Christ wept and was shaken at the tomb of Lazarus. Jesus wept, revealing his human nature and the depth of his love for his friend. From Jesus' perspective, love is the meaning of life. Jesus loves me for what I am, and supports me in my daily efforts to become what God wants me to be, not as the saint I wish I was. As human beings, we all stumble yet, we are loved and destined for life forever in God-in-Christ!

Here is the whole point of our conversation in relationship to the Jubilee Year of Mercy – to be sentinels of mercy like "the dead-bones-sitting" of Rwanda. At the tomb, Jesus with a loud cry commanded Lazarus, *"Lazarus come out!"* After that earth-shaking command and Lazarus coming forth from the grave, Jesus, with a mother's attitude and tone of tender care, handed over the fragile Lazarus to the community for Tender Loving Care, T.L.C.

From "The Terms of Mercy," we can learn at least two lessons. One, the old man drew strength from the life-giving stories of Jesus on the mercy of God and became Christ-like -– *"Blessed are the merciful for they shall obtain mercy"* (Mt. 5:7). Two, the old man's new attitude of merciful-forgiveness is an example of living "the resurrected life." Even now on earth we can live the life we will live forever in heaven. These lessons call us to radical discipleship. In the midst of so much violence, crime, and death, we are called to walk the road less travelled like "the dead-bones-sitting" of Rwanda.

The jury is out. The verdict is loud and clear - as disciples of the Risen Christ, we are challenged to witness even now to the Resurrection life that is not yet. Like the "dead-bones-sitting" of Rwanda, from what grave injustice is Jesus commanding you to settle with healing mercy? Which man or woman, brother or sister, friend, neighbor or colleagues are you called to set free? Thus, like the young man of Rwanda and like Lazarus, they can be re-integrated into the family, the faith community and the wider society. The "Terms of Mercy" is unconditional forgiveness that heals deep wounds, divisions and gives new life.

Lord God,
we thank you for the peace and justice
process in Rwanda.
May the Holy Spirit inspire more men
and women,
in all nations,
with terms of prodigal mercy,
as he did with the "dead-bones-sitting" of
Rwanda.
This is our prayer through our merciful
brother, Jesus Christ. Amen.

Chapter Four. The Appearances of Mercy

To see others as God sees them is easier said than done. This chapter uses the story of the choice of David (1Sam. 16:1, 6-7, 10-13) and the story of the healing of the man born blind (Jn. 9:1-41), to make a case for us to choose the demanding path of faith in judging others.

In Book VII of the Republic, Plato tells a story about men who live all their lives in a Cave[7]. They are chained to pillars and are unable to look back. They can see only shadows cast on the Cave's wall by a fire burning behind them. These men are confident about the power of their eyesight and about their ability to give accurate interpretation to what they see. Yet, all they have been seeing are shadows. One day, one of them breaks free of his chains and makes it outside of the Cave where he sees a whole new world. At first, he is blinded by the light from the real sun, but he gradually adjusts and begins to acquire knowledge of real things. For the first time, he comes to the realization of the absurdity of the "shadow culture of knowledge" of the Cave. On returning into the

Cave, he shares with others, the incredible light by which he saw real things. They not only reject his report, but they resent him and even threaten to kill him.

Let's look at what the Cave of the Prophet Samuel and the Pharisees of Israel can represent. The real world that exists, independent of our human experiences and observations, is the Kingdom of God. Jesus is the incarnate "Sun" through whose light we acquire knowledge of true things. The means to acquiring knowledge through Christ is by faith. In the Gospels Jesus's attempt to reveal his identity and mission to the religious leaders meets a brick wall (Jn. 9:1-41). They attempt to use the man born blind as a scapegoat to vent their rejection and resentment of Jesus.

The man born blind from birth, shows a clear movement of coming from life lived in the shadows to the light of faith and knowledge of Jesus. One sees this in the titles he uses to address Jesus. First, he acknowledges the one who healed him as "the man called Jesus." Next, before the religious leaders, he acknowledges Jesus as "a prophet." And, finally, he makes a profession of faith in Jesus, *"'I do believe, Lord', and he worshipped him."*

Like the story of the men left in the Cave, as the man born blind ascends into light, the sighted religious leaders cling to the shadows and remain in darkness away from the light of faith. The presumption of everyone is that the man was born blind because either he or the parents were sinners. The religious leaders held a livid resentment of the man born blind; *"You were born totally in sin, and are you trying to teach us?"* Their resentment becomes a judgment that denies the man a place with others at communal worship. But Jesus seeks and finds the man born blind and proclaims him and his parents innocent and makes the final determination of the source of the evil, namely, the blindness, rejection and hardness of the human heart: *"If you were blind, you would have no sin; but now that you are saying, 'We see,' your sin remains."*

This narrative is paradoxically titled "The Appearances of Mercy" to challenge the reader/listener to a re-examination of our own cultural context of "political correctness"[8] which could be compared to the "shadow examination" of things in Plato's Cave. We may actually be hiding under language and ignorance in seeing people as they appear to us rather than as God sees them. In the Lenten season that calls us to a change of attitude, our presentation warns us against deep seated human arrogance and high moral grandstanding in our personal and social relationships. It serves the common good to perceive things from God's perspective and to be on the side of Truth. The light of Faith helps us in this matter.

In the story of Samuel, God cautions Samuel not to judge by appearances: *"As they [Jesse and his sons] came, he looked at Eliab and thought, 'Surely the anointed is here before the Lord.' But the Lord said to Samuel: 'Don't judge from appearances … God does not see as a mortal, who sees the appearance. The Lord looks into the Heart'"* (1Sam. 16:6-7). What you see may not be what you get. There is more to see than meets the eye. The heart has eyes that the naked eye has not. Go with your heart in dealing with your own humankind. Then, you will walk by faith in merciful love and not by sight. Faith's insight prompts us to embrace the foresight of St. Paul about the dark side of our common humanity and the need to be merciful: *"You were once darkness, but now you are light in the Lord"* (Eph. 5:8-14). In the light of the same mercy that God sees all of us in Christ, we disciples of Christ, can do no differently.

Lord God, in the many caves of our modern cultures that hide the truth of who we are in Christ, how hard it is for us to see like Jesus? By the grace of the Jubilee Year of Mercy grant us the Light to see as Christ sees all men and women. May we not fear to make enemies in seeking to proclaim and uphold the dignity of us all as your sons and daughters in Christ! Amen

7. Plato's "Republic, Book VII"

8. This is one of those insightful remarks by Mrs. Joann Adams: "Do not only the stuff that we think others would want us to do but do stuff that we think others would like and want us do. To do and behave otherwise means making enemies; but hopefully more friends than enemies."

Chapter Five. The Missionaries of Mercy

In our modern age of globalization the Church invites us to become disciples of the "New Evangelization." What is the New Evangelization? According to Pope Emeritus Benedict XVI, the New Evangelization is, *"re-proposing the Gospel to those regions awaiting the first evangelization and to those regions where the roots of Christianity are deep but who have experienced a serious crisis of faith due to secularization."*[9] We who have been evangelized are called to renew our faith in the gospel message and become evangelizers to others. With the text of John's story of the Samaritan woman at the well, this chapter on "Missionaries of Mercy" calls us to turn inwards, deepen our relationship with Jesus, in readiness for the New Evangelization (Jn. 4:5-42).

The gospel story of the encounter between Jesus and the Samaritan Woman is here retold to make it our personal and communal storylines about the identity of Jesus as God's

Self-revealing Word made flesh (Jn. 1:1, 14). I retell it with emphasis on its deep human appeal. At the outset, Jesus does a very human thing by initiating a human conversation: *"Hello there woman, do you mind if I drink from your cup?"* *Imagine the woman's surprise, "Really, do you mean from another cup or from my cup?"*

Does this ring a bell of how sometimes we seek each other's attention? With this ice breaker attitude, Jesus makes an impression on the un-named woman who now becomes the face of all Samaritans. Why? Because Samaritans and Jews who knew the traditional attitudes, the politics and social norms of these two groups of people, knew the rules that governed their interactions in private and in public --- they simply avoided each other! But this gentleman called Jesus, a learned Jew, obviously knew the rules but breaks the rules[10]. He associates with a person from an unfriendly nation. And not just that, he engages a woman in a caring manner without any concern about what his disciples or the passers-by or anyone else would say.

The woman, seems to like attention grabbers, out-going types, and Jesus seems one of the unique ones that sweep ladies feet off the ground. So she does a very human thing by opening up to the encounter; like Jesus, she cares less for rules and engages this man in her own way. From addressing him *"a Jew"* at the outset, she moves to a personable level and addresses him as *"Sir!"* She perceives something different about Jesus, *"Begins to believe,"* and a personal relationship develops.

From the personal human level, the conversation moves to the level of God-talk. Both know their faith traditions so they share the word of God on "Living flowing Water and gift of God." The woman acknowledges Jacob's well as the source of their living water, but Jesus states that he is the water of eternal life. Now that she has met her seventh *"Man,"*[11], the woman asks her man for a favor: *"give me this water."* From addressing Jesus as Sir, she progresses to *"Prophet"* and reaches the divine truth, *"I know that the Messiah is coming, the one called the Christ; when he comes, he will tell us everything."* At that point, Jesus reveals himself, *"I am he, the one speaking to you"*.

For the second time, the Samaritan woman is swept off the ground, but this time in divine awe, finding herself in the presence of God's self-revealing Word made flesh. On her own, she becomes a missionary. Returning home she gives her missionary testament to her fellow Samaritans. Through her testimony, some of her townspeople are moved to find out things for themselves. On meeting Jesus, they too become co-missionaries, winning Jesus over to accompany them to Samaria for a greater audience of their townspeople. Jesus arrives and stays with the Samaritans, who like their daughter at the well, have their own personal encounter with Jesus. Their eventual profession of faith in Jesus, evokes our own too, *"We ... have heard ... we know that this is truly the savior of the world."*

What lessons can we draw, from the beautiful divine- human story of the Samaritan woman, for the implementation of the agenda of the New Evangelization, which has been presented by Pope Emeritus Benedict XVI? Three lessons stand out from the story. One, like the

Samaritan woman, encountering Jesus makes one feel special and makes one want to become a better human person. Two, it makes one want to get to know him more as a trusted friend who accepts people as they are. Three, it makes one long to follow him and even become his "sales man or woman," to tell of the good news of the Kingdom of God. Practically, therefore, these lessons can help us "re-propose the gospel" as follows: To those regions awaiting primary evangelization, they present Jesus as one who shares the intimacy of our common humanity; He is a divine person who leads us to our eternal destiny in God. And very importantly, they call the Church, as the Body of Christ, to conversion on its past and present biases against people and groups, especially, the separated Christian Churches and other Faith Traditions.

In our modern age of globalization, the story of the Samaritan woman challenges us to rediscover our common humanity and dignity in God-in-Christ; and with other Christians it inspires us to become authentic "Missionaries of Mercy."

Prayer of Pope Frances for the Jubilee Year of Mercy:

Lord Jesus Christ,

You have taught us to be merciful like the heavenly Father, and have told us that whoever sees you sees Him. Show us your face and we will be saved.

Your loving gaze freed Zacchaeus and Matthew from being enslaved by money;

The adulteress and Magdalene from seeking happiness only in created things;

Made Peter weep after betrayal, and assured Paradise to the repentant thief.

Let us hear, as if addressed to each one of us, the words that you spoke to the Samaritan woman:

"If you knew the Gift of God!"

We ask this of you, Lord Jesus, through the intercession of Mary, Mother of Mercy, you who live and reign with the Father and the Holy Spirit for ever and ever. Amen.

9. Pope Benedict XVI, "Homily of First Vespers on the Solemnity of Apostles Peter and Paul." The Vatican http://www.vatican.va/holyfather/benedictxvihomilies/2010/documents/hfben-xvihom20100628vespri-pietro-paoloent.html

10. The traditional attitude is to "stay within the box"; people do not like it when you "go outside the box."

11. Recall that the woman had five men already in her life. She was living with the sixth man. Jesus, to whom she has opened up her heart and being, becomes the seventh man.

Chapter Six. The Infinity of Mercy

This is the story of how the organization, *"Medecins San Frontieres/Doctors Without Borders, (MSF)"[12]* began, making it eminently a model for "The Infinity of Mercy." During the Nigerian civil war (1967-1970), the Federal Nigerian government blockaded the Eastern territory, thus preventing much needed humanitarian aids from reaching the people. While most of the world turned to look the other way so as not to see *"Quashokow"[13]*, starved children and bleeding men and women with no medical care, a few became the conscience of humankind. On January 11, 1971, leaders on both sides of the conflict signed an agreement to mark the end of the tragic war. By December 20, 1971, brave human hearts stood up to the world with a new vision for human rights and dignity.

In Paris, a group of French doctors and journalists who had witnessed the unconscionable inhuman conditions resulting from the Nigerian government's actions, vowed in the name of all humankind, never again to turn away from any human suffering, no matter the danger in any war situation. They resolved to process a new path in care for people in war torn situations regardless of borders. Their vision was inspired by the belief that all peoples have the right to medical care regardless of race, religion, creed, or political affiliation; that peoples' needs are more important than national borders. These were apolitical sentiments from people quite respectful of our world's political perspectives. They spoke from their hearts to all hearts, for all times, beyond all borders.

In 2016, forty-five years after its founding, MSF provides medical aid to people in over seventy countries of our world. The visionary echoes of the seers, prophets, professionals, and volunteers of MSF ring incessantly true today beyond borders, in the cauldron clanks and clatters of our war-torn global village of the 21st century. The Lukan story of the beginning of Jesus' Galilean ministry and his rejection in Nazareth is my text for reflection (Lk. 4:24-30). It should sensitize us to the vision of our new world order that is struggling with the problem of national borders, migration and refugees fleeing from war torn nations.

For those whose life's journey is guided by faith in the God-man Jesus Christ of Nazareth, they would embrace the vision and mission of MSF as grounded in the organic gospel message that God's favor is beyond the borders of Galilee, *"The Spirit of the Lord is upon me, because he has anointed me to bring good news to the poor. He has sent me to proclaim liberty to captives and recovery of sight to the blind, to let the oppressed go free, and to proclaim a year acceptable to the Lord" (Lk. 4: 18-19).* Those outside the borders of Galilee (or in our own small worlds) are part and parcel of God's plan, and most importantly, are all sons and daughters of God. The poignant words of Jesus to his indignant home crowd that: *"no prophet is accepted at home,"* is an *aporia*, an expression of inexpressible doubt.

In the minds of those who cannot see beyond borders, this phenomenal unfolding cascades God's message of healing truth, hope, and mercy that is ahead of space and time. God's healing message will waste away in the violence of our world if seers, prophets, professionals, and volunteers of all shapes and hues, stay home when there are people screaming for human and humane renewal and restoration.

The critical message of Jesus is from his sacred heart whose boundaries are equidistant with infinity. Acting from his heart, he goes on to walk the heart-talk of seers, prophets, professionals, and volunteers of infinity in the face of public outrage and violence. A challenge, indeed, to us with hearts, perhaps closed to seeing the miseries of the new exodus of people fleeing from homes and nations they may never see again. Dare to open up your infinite hearts to an Infinite God of Mercy. Like the doctors, nurses, and volunteers of Medecins san Fronteires, Christian disciples of all ages and peoples of goodwill of all ages must be people with hearts without borders. Like the ancient troubadours who invented songs to express love, members of Medecins san Fronteires, in our day, are troubadours who create radical paths that welcome people, from North and South, East and West, into the depths of God's healing love by their compassionate deeds. In the Jubilee year of Mercy, in our wounded world, all lovers of humanity must become radical hearts open to the radical grace of the Lord of Infinity of "Mercy san frontiers."

Risen Lord of Infinite Mercy,
cause to blossom in us an infinity of
particles
of spiritual waves and winds of Mercy
for missions without borders.
With incarnate faith may we become as
you are,
see as you see and love as you love.
May we imagine a world actively healing
in God's love.
May your kingdom of Mercy be realized
in our wounded world
because we dared to dream and act as
you do ··· beyond borders!
Amen.

12. MSF, Medecins Sans Fronteires is French for Doctors without Borders.
13. *Quashokaw* is sickness that results from lack of food and proper feeding.

Chapter Seven. The Time for Mercy

In his memorable song of the 1960s, *"Turn! Turn! Turn!"* Pete Seeger draws from King Solomon's timeless insight about the inscrutability of human worldly acts in fourteen pairs of opposites:

There is an appointed time for everything, and a time for every human affair under the heavens.
A time to give birth and a time to die; a time to plant and a time to uproot the plant.
A time to kill and a time to heal; a time to tear down and a time to build.
A time to weep and a time to laugh; a time to mourn and a time to dance.
A time to scatter stones and a time to gather them; a time to embrace and a time to be far from embraces.
A time to seek and a time to lose; a time to keep and a time to cast away.
A time to rend and a time to sew; a time to be silent and a time to speak.
A time to love and a time to hate; a time of war and a time of peace (Ecclesiastes 3:1-8).

To King Solomon's digest, Pete adds a provocative line: *"A time for peace I swear it's not too late!"* And in our own global context, we can add with insistence: *"A time to fast for mercy, it's time to reconcile for merciful peace!"* Note the centrality of time in these schematic lines. In this reflection, we ponder its three ecstasies of: time past and time future in the attentive acts of time present. The word that takes in all three ecstasies is *"NOW"* – a word that configures all and gives us wisdom to light our way on the journey of life.

In the Jubilee Year of Mercy, the Church challenges people of faith and men and women of goodwill to become "Missionaries of Mercy". The time of the Church's challenge couldn't be more appropriate than during the Christian Lenten season of prayer, fasting, and almsgiving. To meet the Church's challenge, we draw inspiration from Prophet Joel (2:12-18), St. Paul (2 Cor 5:20-6:2), and the Gospel of Mathew (6:1-6, 16-18).

Prophet Joel, 450 years before Christ, proclaimed to the people: *"Even now, says the Lord, return to me with your whole heart, with fasting, and weeping and mourning"* (Joel 2:12). St. Paul, 2000 years ago, proclaimed a similar message to the people: *"Be reconciled to God ... Behold now is the acceptable time, behold now is the day of salvation"* (2Cor. 5:20, 6:2) Joel uses *"Now"* once while Paul uses it twice in the texts cited. With it, both have been able to bring space and time into space-time, thus transforming the past into the present.

In the gospel, Jesus gives us three practical ways for Christian living *"Now"*: prayer, fasting, and almsgiving. Because these traditional practices are meant to transform us inwardly to be-come better friends and followers, Jesus commands us not to play politics with them by "trumpeting" them to impress people. We must avoid "sound bites" as much as possible. In place of "grandstanding" Jesus further commands us to, *"Wash your face, so that you may not appear to be fasting"* (Mt. 6:17-18).

What do we mean then by putting ashes on our foreheads on Ash Wednesday? Sometimes do they not make us look funny wearing the black marks on our foreheads like some kind of talisman? Why do we go public with those black marks on our foreheads? Are we hypocrites? Not necessarily, if at all! They serve both as symbols as well as metaphors.

37

We go public with ashes on our foreheads as a visible commitment to be faithful witnesses to gospel values in daily living. Hopefully, as the day and our ashes disappear, our resolve to continue to be bearers of unconditional merciful love, continues.

Therefore, fellow Missionaries of Mercy, let our Lenten metanoia[14] be seen "Now" in our practical merciful deeds for the other(s). To keep our commitment, behold time further beckons: like Prophet Joel and St. Paul even *"Now"*, to whom do you wholeheartedly believe you are sent as a missionary of Mercy? Even *"Now"*, what can your prayer, fasting and almsgiving do to give life to that other person(s)? Even now, Mercy Incarnate, Jesus Christ, beckons to you, to us! Like Pete Seeger, I swear it, a time for mercy is not too late! And with King Solomon I definitely believe that: *"Now"*, it is our time to reconcile for merciful peace.

14. *Metanoia* is a spiritual conversion that affects one's core being and attitude. It is a kind of change that compares to turning around 360%.

Chapter Eight. The Economy of Mercy

The world economy is going through a massive transition right now. The knowledge economy is the future. By bringing everyone online, we'll not only improve billions of lives, but we'll also improve our own as we benefit from their ideas and productivity they contribute to the world. Giving everyone the opportunity to connect is the foundation for enabling the knowledge economy (Mark Elliot Zuckerberg in his Facebook post, August, 2013).

In raising the subject of "The Economy of Mercy", the presumption is that Mercy, as an economy of living relationships in our century, is in decline. If you say it is not true, then I'll lay the burden of proof to the contrary on you, my reader-listeners by telling your own stories of deeds of mercy. In telling of your own experiences, others would draw inspiration to cultivate an economy of mercy improving billions of lives. "The Economy of Mercy", in this context, is a metaphor for the *"Struggle to restore Mercy and those who burn the midnight candle to restore the culture of mercy in our world."* (The emphasis is mine). The question is why does it not come natural to us to be cultivators of mercy? Mark Elliot Zuckerberg helps us answer that question from his stellar Facebook story as reported in Wikipedia, the free encyclopedia.

Zuckerberg is a Jewish-American internet great and philanthropist. He is a co-founder of Facebook, a website for social networking. Early in middle school, he began playing around with computers, eventually becoming a noted computer software developer. With some friends in college and at Harvard University, he launched Facebook. In August 2013, from Facebook, he launched the Internet.org project, with the purpose of providing internet services to billions of people not connected to the global internet highway. Through this internet project, he created new jobs and opened new markets guided by the vision statement quoted above. More than the pursuit of wealth for personal indulgence, Zuckerberg and his wife Priscilla, have been loyal to their shared intention to serve global humanity. In October 2014, both donated $25 million to fight the Ebola Virus pandemic in West Africa.

In 2012, they promised to give more than half of their wealth to *"advancing human potential and promoting equality" in the spirit of "The Giving People"* [15] *(Wikipedia report under Philanthropy).* To mark the birth of their daughter Maxima (Max), on December 1, 2015, they pledged, over the course of their lives, to give 99 percent of their Facebook shares to the Chan Zuckerberg Initiative, with focus on health and education. The point of this conversation is that Mark Zuckerberg is an extraordinary missionary of mercy in his own right. With an uncommon grace at such a youthful age, he has become a benefactor in the service of global human good. He might be one of the leading philanthropists in our world today.

But, for his intellectual wizardry and for the wealth at his command, he has paid a great price in order to bear so many personal and public fruits. He has burned the proverbial 'midnight candle' and our world has become a better place for his efforts. With Thomas Edison, Mark Zuckerberg can say that *"Genius is one percent inspiration and ninety nine percent perspiration."* Indeed for them failure is a synonym for a million ways to success. *They never say never till never is ever Eureka!*

In the canon of religious language, perspiration is a metaphor for Patience. And one can qualify it as "patient-struggle." The fruit of patient-struggle in the economy of mercy is compassionate deeds. And inspiration is a gift of God scripted in our DNAs.

Here is where Jesus comes in with his parable of the barren fig-tree (Lk. 13:1-9) to challenge individuals and religious leaders to work towards recreating mercy in our world. For us all, God is the Master-Gardener, ever patient and ready to give each tree (symbolizing human beings), one more chance to bear fruit. In a special way, our Christian faith gives us a deeper understanding of our call as collaborators with God, the Master Gardener. Therefore we have the greater responsibility to call others to work as co-gardeners with God. Together we must seek out, in our world, people needing "Tender Loving Care -TLC" in order to bear fruits of mercy.

To religious leaders the challenge to be zealous co-gardeners with God-in-Christ is most urgent in the Jubilee Year of Mercy. Their members look up to them to produce not just any type of fruits but quality fruits. God gives them another chance to be renewed and grow in mercy. In the spirit of being God's children, Jesus challenges us all to look out into our world to see how it struggles for nourishing fruits of mercy. Zuckerberg and other "Giving People" are good examples of those who have responded to the challenge of Jesus. We cannot do differently. *Never say never until never is ever Eureka!* Take responsibility for the "One percent" inspiration to yield the abundant fruits of mercy to replenish the dwindling stock of mercy in our century. At this point, the question is no more, "Why doesn't the cultivation of mercy flow naturally from us?" The real question is, "how do we cultivate the Economy of Mercy in our own Lives?" Now that the world economy is in massive transition, together with the Knowledge Economy, the Economy of Mercy is our real human and humane future.

Bless the lord, O my soul, and all within me,
bless his holy name!
Bless the Lord, O my soul, and never forget all his benefits. ...
It is the Lord who ... crowns you with mercy and compassion,
and fills your life with good things, renewing your life like an eagle's (Psalm 103:1-2, 4-5).
Amen

15. "The Giving People" are a group of individuals who have embraced the "Giving Pledge Campaign" that encourages wealthy people of the world to give their net worth of the wealth to Philanthropy. The Giving Pledge campaign began in June 2010 with Bill Gates and Warren Buffet as pioneers. In April, 2016 "Insatiable Fox" media reported that 139 individuals worldwide have joined the 'The Giving People.' Within the context of the vision of "Flickers of Mercy," the giving people are Missionaries of Mercy. To their poverty of spirit the Beatitudes proclaim, "Blessed are the merciful for they shall obtain mercy" (Mt. 5:7).

Chapter Nine. The Home of Mercy

In the summer of 1996, I had an opportunity of a life-time: to attend a series of courses on *"Peace Building, Religious Leadership, and Conflict Resolution"* at the University of West Virginia, USA. The star lecturer for me, and many other participants, was an American Jewish professor. At every lecture of his, one could see and feel sparks of intelligence lighting the entire lecture hall and moving us from self into self-forgetfulness. The question we asked was: "Who is this intriguing man? What tradition formed and set him on this awesome path of *illuminata* with such humbleness?" A learned, wise and committed teacher he was indeed!

The answer came when the professor told us that he was a practicing Jew. Every Friday, he would hurry home to be in readiness for the observance of the Sabbath with his wife and children. As I recall, he said while his Sabbath lasted, all modern, cultural conveniences were put aside. He shared that Sabbath was, *"..... life lived as prescribed in the Torah. The Torah is like a home we always long to return to; where discords mend into accords; where brokenness bows to wholeness; where the elements in nature in wedlock with the human spirit configure peace. The Torah is not a burden; it is a brother and a sister; it is a true guide and guard for waking and sleeping on the journey of life."*

The learned professor drew strength for total commitment to the laws of Yahweh. He made a proactive choice for a life lived in the *illuminata*[16] of the Lord God and showed his wife and children the easiest way to lasting peace (Deut. 30:15-20). Christians, like their Jewish brothers, sisters and ancestors, make a choice for the Law of the Lord written in their hearts and given by their new Moses, Jesus the Christ. His law is a paradox. He not only shows us the way to peace, he is the Way and Peace. He not only tells the Truth, he is the Truth. He not only radiates healing light, he is the *Illuminata*.

All leads us into the context of life in our world and the search for elusive Lady Peace. Look at the world stage: Do you see any chances of peace-ability? In the uneasy and numbing, confused and confusing living experiences of

today, in the midst of trending terror and
crimes, in the specter of the new exodus and
daily escalating wars, even in the region of the
birth-place of Peace-incarnate, our world longs
for peace. Around us, in the midst of mourning
the loss of a dear husband, wife, son, daughter,
father, mother, or friend, Christ defiantly dares
us to trust in him as the true home where
concord mends discord and loving mercy
makes us whole again (Lk. 9:22-25).

The Cross is everywhere! Life is a cross!
Between symbol and metaphor there seems to
be no difference and no choice. But Christ
beckons us insistently *"Take up your cross daily
and follow me."* Jesus, our new Torah, isn't a
burden. He is a brother and best friend who
sets us free. In His other home – the Mystical
Body of Christ, the Church – in Him, through
Him and with Him who sets us free, we can see
things differently as in *"a mirror darkly."* In the
midst of sadness, we can celebrate. Christ is
our joy and *illuminata* of hope. *"And blessed
are those who hope in the Lord!"* (PS. 40:5)

I have come to experience the Church of St.
Pius X as that other home to return to, where
the Law of the heart in Christ is celebrated,

with gusto, every Sabbath and every morning, by the members, for the members, and with the members, to mend discordance into concordance and keep hope alive in those stressed in distress. In the context of this other home in Tucson, where the new Torah, Jesus, the Way, the Truth and the Life palpably reigns, I have had the audacity to celebrate the life of the young radiant   light, PJ Farrell. He celebrated his first heavenly birthday as we, the Farrell family, friends and faith community of St. Pius X celebrated his nineteenth earthly-birthday in time.

Oh God of our homes,
in the midst of our lingering pains of loss,
let your healing light of hope help us to engage
in the celebrations of the eternal Paschal dance,
as we, in our other home of your merciful healing and truth,
draw strength for the journey home in Christ.
Amen

16. *Illuminata* has its root in *Illuminatio*, meaning to illuminate. It is used here with theological intent to express our relationship to God "Who is Light itself." God is the fullness or totality of light. And we, *illuminata,* particles of God's light, are alight in God, our Light. The opening line of Psalm 27 says *"Diominus illuminatio" – "The Lord is my light"!*

Chapter Ten. The Transfiguration of Mercy

Today in our world, with unprecedented terrorist attacks resulting in countless deaths, God's divine presence appears lacking compared to the stories of dramatic divine-human encounter in Genesis 15:5-12; and in the story of the Transfiguration in Luke 9:28-36. In this chapter we seek to reassure ourselves of God's presence in our midst through our compassionate deeds.

We begin with a brief statistics on terrorism from the year 2000 to the beginning of 2016. On November 17, 2015, Matt Chorley, in the *Daily Mail* Newspaper report, revealed that terrorist attacks and deaths, from the year 2000 to the year 2014, increased nine-fold. In 2014 alone, deaths from terrorist attacks worldwide increased by 80%, prompting a surge in the number of refugees fleeing from their homes and countries. In 2015, four major attacks in Beirut, Paris, Nigeria and Mali raised questions about the new levels of global terrorism. At the beginning of 2016, two media events rattled the United States and the

International Community. Within the United States, on February 9, the Director of National Intelligence, James Clapper, warned that Isis may directly attack the US Homeland in 2016. On the International level, on February 10, in its editorial comment, the *Chicago Tribune* raised a damming alarm on the new level of carnage in Syria, especially in its biggest city of Aleppo, calling it a humanitarian crisis at its worst.

In reflecting on the above statistics, and considering the number of lives lost to global terrorism, one may not be wrong in calling our world, "A Traumatized and Fearful World." One may even be tempted to raise some troubling questions about God's relationship to our world: *"Why does God allow evil on such a massive scale in our world? Is there a trace of light at the end of the tunnel?"* Do these questions represent false alarms about the reality of fear in our world? No, not really, because they affirm the confused state of our world, our helplessness and our need for divine intervention.

As people of faith we are asked to consider what we can do to bring about peaceful coexistence. Like Abram, in the difficult situation of our world, we must turn from doubt and despair to faith and action: *"Abram put his faith in the Lord, who attributed it to him as an act of righteousness"* (Gen. 15:6). In an earlier encounter, God had promised Abram a great nation and through him a blessing to all the nations of the earth. But reaching old age with no child, Abram despairs that he would die without an heir. God reaches out and makes a promise to Abram. This time, Abram asks for a reassuring sign. To make a long story, short, Abram is keeping watch. It is at that point that *"a deep, terrifying darkness enveloped him."* Abram enters into a trance and experiences God's passing close (15:12-16). Notice the paradox of the divine presence in the midst of fear and death.

In the Gospel during the transfiguration of Jesus, Luke reports that Peter, James and John, who had been overcome by sleep, became fully awake when they saw two men [Moses and Elijah] standing with Jesus. But, towards the end of the transfiguration *"they became frightened"* [as] *"a cloud came and cast a shadow over them"* (Lk. 9:28-36). There followed the eruption of the divine in *"a voice that said, 'This is my chosen son, listen to him.'"* Notice again the presence of the divine in the midst of fear.

In these instances God, in His pre-eminent wisdom, re-figures and transfigures fear and death into faith and a covenant relationship with His own. To Abram's quest for re-assurance, God promises him a homeland from *"the Wadi of Egypt to the Great River, the Euphrates"*, for endless generations.

In our world, where the evil of terrorism seems impossible to overcome, the Church challenges us to renew our faith in God-in-Christ. By our prayer, fasting and almsgiving during Lent, and beyond Lent, we can transfigure the world starting from the little corners of our villages, towns and cities.

What are we challenged to do ourselves in response to the transfiguration question in our daily lives particularly during Lent? We are called to reflect, contemplate, and act on a transfiguration of our own in a prayerful mood in imitation of Jesus who *"went up the mountain to pray."* On what subject are we to proactively reflect and contemplate? Simply, on the mission of God's "Chosen Son" in His compassionate deeds. Pope Francis has given us, in "Authentic Fasting that Leads to Blessings" a way to re-configure both Isaiah's and Jesus' ways of compassion:

... releasing those bound unjustly, untying the thongs of the yoke, setting free the oppressed, breaking off every yoke,... sharing your bread with the hungry, ... bringing the afflicted and the homeless into your house, clothing the naked when you see them and not turning your back on your own flesh ... remove the yoke from among you, the accusing finger and the malicious speech ... lavishing your food on the hungry and satisfying the afflicted; then your light shall rise in the darkness. And you shall be like a watered garden, like a flowing spring whose waters never fail (Isaiah 58:6-7, 9-11).

How we reconfigure the above details is totally our business. To aid us in the process, here are some enabling suggestions:

1. Can you, in trusting supplication, turn over to God, in prayer, the fears and deaths in our nation, in the world, in your own heart?

2. Can you proactively reflect and make the compassionate deeds of the Suffering Servant your short and long term project?
3. How and to whom will you become a catalyst of living mercy to incarnate a living experience of mercy in the person(s) around you?

Lord God,
may our prayer, fasting and almsgiving
transfigure the fears and deaths of our
brothers and sisters
within and beyond our borders,
into life-giving experiences
through the passion and death of Jesus
Christ!
Through us may Jesus' transfiguration
become a living "Transfiguration of
Mercy!"
Amen.

Chapter Eleven. The Eucharistta of Mercy

In the Christian liturgy of Holy Thursday, the washing of the feet takes center stage with good reason, for it holds the meaning of Christ's command: *"As I have done, you should also do" (Jn. 13:15)*. The command gives us an idea but the practice of it brings home the message. Within the practice of that command, I have two human experiences to bring the message home and send each of you on the mission of mercy.

The first experience took place while I was about to pay my bill at the shopping place in town. I was pretty sure I had enough cash on me until the cashier gave me the actual cost of my purchase. I knew at that point that I hadn't enough money with me. "I am short of cash, I will rush home and I will be back," I said to the lady with a sense of self-disappointment. Just at that moment, I heard a voice behind me say, "I have some coupons for that, how much is it?" Turning, I saw a lady smiling and thank God, her smile took away my awkward feeling. Then she drew nearer and said to me,

"Seriously, how much do you need, you don't need to go home!" Reluctantly I told her what I needed, and she reached into her bag and brought out cash instead of coupons. As I handed the money over to the cashier, her face brightened into a smile fixed on my angel behind me.

That rescue angel might have been at the solemn Holy Thursday liturgy that I celebrated. But, whether she was there or not, does not matter. Even now I pay tribute to Evelyn, who paid the balance of my bill. At the time I got stuck, her eyes looked smiling at me. In turning around, my eyes, shrouded in shame and self-pity, looked at her smiling eyes, and the feeling was mutual. *"Sometimes things do not work out as we plan them. Trust me I have been in your kind of shoes before. I was helped by an angel, so I am your angel this afternoon,"* she seemed to say. What wonder that woman's heart performed!

What surprise mercy has for the simple and trusting! Whenever, wherever, and whoever will read this text, I proclaim a memorial in merciful gratitude: *"I thank you Evelyn, everly! Forever, you have given me and a multitude another perfect example to follow. At the Holy Thursday liturgical celebration, you not only gave me what to preach but you also taught me concretely the meaning of: 'As I have done... you should also do.'"*

The second experience involves Pope Francis, who on his first Holy Thursday celebration as Pope, knelt down to wash a woman's feet in an Italian prison. He was then 77 years old. I can only imagine the awkward feeling of an old man struggling to kneel down to do the master's command - OUCH! These two contrasting human experiences, follow Jesus' perfect example and command: "As I have done... you should also do." Both examples have become for me extended metaphors for service to others in need. But there is an ambiguity in the scripture readings that challenges us about the double character of the type of service to others that is required of us.

The reading from Exodus, describes the Jewish Passover feast which we Christians see as a foreshadowing of our Eucharistic celebration (Ex. 12:1-8, 11-14). In the Letter to the Corinthians, St. Paul recalls for us, Jesus our eternal Passover who is our Eucharistic Paschal Lamb of sacrifice which, "*I received … I also handed on to you, bread blessed, broken, and shared; and cup blessed, poured, and shared*" (Paraphrasing is mine). Christ is the bread of life given to strengthen our broken bodies in the service of others. The wine is the blood of Jesus given as a tonic to nudge us to pour out our lives in the service of others. What we do is "*In remembrance … and proclamation of the death of the Lord until he comes*" (1 Cor.11:23-26).

Next, notice the seeming ambiguity that comes with the gospel of John on the occasion of the Institution of the Eucharist. Instead of the narrative of the institution of the Eucharist, we rather have a basin of water, a towel, and the disciples' feet to wash (Jn. 13:1-15). There is a theological lesson for all to learn and live its message. The washing of the feet is an outward sign that reveals the grace of the Eucharist. On every occasion of the celebration of the Institution of the Eucharist, Jesus teaches us that those who wash the feet of others manifest God's gift in them. In washing the feet of others they serve God in them. And those who serve the needs of others, in keeping with the Lord's command, are called "Eucharistta."

Like my angel at the shopping center and Pope Francis washing the feet of the woman at the prison, I invite you to become, in the Jubilee Year of Mercy, "The Eucharistta of Mercy." Jesus has given us a perfect example to follow: *"As I have done... you should also do."* Like Jesus in the Eucharist that is broken and shared for us how do you become Eucharist broken and shared for others? How will you wash another's feet always? In washing another's feet you will understand the real meaning of the Institution of the Eucharist. Washing another's feet is, obtaining double blessedness, adoring Jesus in the Eucharist and Jesus present in others.

Lord God,
by the power of the Holy Spirit
endow us with the strength and vigor
to become a Eucharistic people.
In serving others,
may we adore you,
our bread of life and our cup of salvation.
Through Christ our Lord. Amen.

Chapter Twelve. The Veil of Mercy

On Easter Sunday, Mother Church bids us celebrate the good news of the resurrection of Jesus Christ with joyful mercy: *Give thanks to the Lord, for he is good, for his mercy endures forever.* And our response to the Church's invitation is: *This is the day that the Lord has made; let us rejoice and be glad or simply Alleluia! (Psalm 118).* But our joy, even on the day of our festival, must be measured for good reasons. Two of those reasons I share with you.

First, in 2009, Asia Bibi, a Pakistani Christian, mother of five was imprisoned, accused of blasphemy. According to a recent news report, she is now on death row. Her only "crime," according to the report, was offering water to her Muslim co-worker from the same cup out of which she, a Christian, had drank. The good news is that the Supreme Court of Pakistan ordered the stay of her execution while reviewing her death sentence. For the stay of execution order in favor of Asia Bibi, we rejoice and say *"Alleluia!"*

Second, early in the year 2016, the Knights of Columbus in partnership with an NGO, "In Defense of Christians (IDC)," submitted a 280 page report to the United States Secretary of State, John Kerry, titled: "Genocide against Christians in the Middle East". Its executive summary states: *"ISIS is committing genocide – the crime of crimes- against Christians and other religious groups in Syria, Iraq, and Libya. It is time for the United States to join the rest of the world by naming it and by taking action against it as required by law."* On March 17, 2016, the United States, having listened to the plea of John Kerry, issued a statement: *"The genocide against Christians, the Yazidis and others is not only a grave injustice to these ancient faith communities – it is an assault on human dignity and an attack on civilization itself. The United States has now spoken with clarity and moral authority."*[17]

With the persecuted Christians around the world, especially in the Middle East, and for the clarity and moral leadership of the United States, we say, *"Alleluia!"* And, while we celebrate the ultimate victory over death by the power of the merciful love of Jesus Christ, the Risen Lord, we must not forget to mercifully reach out to our fellow Christians as they carry their own crosses of persecution. In the spirit of the resurrection narrative, we must, as much as is within our power, assist them in taking off the veil of persecution that prevents them from seeing the face of the risen Lord (Jn. 20:1-9). In place of the veil of persecution, ours is the responsibility, in the Jubilee Year of Mercy, to offer them the "Veil of Mercy" of the Risen Lord. The wisdom of the veil of mercy, contained in the scriptures, urges us on mission in earnest in our maturing but broken world.

In the gospel of John, a woman of mercy, Mary of Magdala, was deeply concerned at the disappearance of the body of Jesus from the tomb. With a heavy heart, sorrowful Mary told Peter and the beloved disciple: *"They have taken the Lord from the tomb, and we don't know where they put him."* Who are the "they" that Mary had in mind? Could it be the government officials that Pilate gave permission to take the body of Jesus from the cross for burial? If they were Joseph of Arimathea and Nicodemus, two men of mercy, then the Lord's body was in safe hands. Like Mary, Joseph and Nicodemus were only doing a kind deed for the one who, after their respective personal encounters with Jesus, transformed them into merciful disciples.

In Mary of Magdala, Joseph of Arimathea, and Nicodemus, therefore, we find models of merciful hearts unlike the religious leaders, the trained-to-kill-soldiers, the brutal Pontius Pilate, the confused Peter, and the disciples who looked the other way on Good Friday. In our own day, one may ask, "Who are 'the' they?" They could be the accusers of Asia Bibi and the members of the Pakistani Supreme Court. They could also be the persecutors of Christians around the world. They could be leaders of modern nations who, like Pilate, know the truth but lack the courage to do the truth. They could even be me and you, in our willed choices and weaknesses, wearing different veils with multitudes of colors and shades.

This is where we seek the intervention of the Risen Lord to remove from us and our world the uncanny multitude of veils of evil and death and, in their stead, unleash the powerful veil of his merciful love to transform us and our world. What is the nature of the Risen Lord's merciful veil?

When Jesus raised Lazarus from death, his face was "wrapped in a cloth." With a firm command, Jesus ordered the grave diggers to, *"Untie him and let him go"* (Jn. 11:44). But in the case of Jesus at his tomb, a game changer took place. According to Peter and the beloved disciples', *"the burial cloths and the cloth that had covered his head (were not in the same place), but rolled up in a separate place."* Mary of Magdala, at the time she made her report to Peter and John, was actually too confused and too grieved to know the truth of what took place at the tomb. Burdened by the pain of loss of Jesus her dear friend, it never crossed her mind that nobody had taken his body away. The truth was that Jesus, the hound of heaven, had unbound himself and gone free. The game-changer for Peter and John was the cloth that had veiled the face of Jesus. It was the same cloth that unveiled their eyes to see, know and believe that the Lord had risen, even without seeing him face to face.

A local proverb says: *"Okut nkpo ke enyin enye ofiok mbuk. Nting nno iko enye oworo nsu - Seeing a thing by oneself, one can tell the true story. A reported story tells half-truth."* For Peter and John, eye witnesses, the evidence was there and complete (Jn.20:8-9). They told of what they saw, not what was told to them. *Finito!* What about Joseph of Arimathea and Nicodemus? Were they among the first few to hear of the eye witness account? Whose account did they believe? Mary's or that of Peter and John? And what about us? Whose witness account appeals to us most? Is it that of Mary or that of Peter and John? Either way do the "eye witness account" make sense at all to us? Here Peter and the beloved disciple and Mary leave us all to reflect and contemplate the question and the meaning of the empty tomb. Our urgent challenge, like that of Mary, Peter and John, remains -- to be on our mission of uncovering the eyes of our fellow men and women, so they may see, know, and believe our Resurrection witness.

In this Jubilee Year of Mercy, can you become the veil of mercy of the Risen Lord? Can you join others like the Knights of Columbus in pledging to stop Christian genocide? Can you pray that Jesus' merciful love may touch the hearts of members of the Supreme Court of Pakistan to reconcile Asia Bibi, indeed reconcile, with the various faith traditions who suffer. And, concretely, how will you let God's mercy be unveiled by others through your deeds of mercy?

Lord God,
may the veils of
religious extremism, fundamentalism,
bigotry, injustice, exclusion, hate and sin
in our world be removed
by the ultimate power of the victory
of Christ's merciful love over evil and
death.
May the veil that covers our eyes
from seeing the truth of everyone's
human dignity
as sons and daughters of God
be removed by our hard-fought and
heart-grown merciful deeds!
Through Christ our Risen Lord!
Amen.

17. "Our Sunday Visitor", Newsweekly, OSV.com; Knights of Columbus website: www.stopthechristiangenocide.org

Chapter Thirteen. Signs and Wonders of Mercy

"Many signs and wonders were done among the people at the hands of the apostles. They were all together in Solomon's portico. None of the others dared to join them, but the people esteemed them. Yet, more than ever, believers in the Lord, great numbers of men and women, were added to them" (Acts 5:12-14).

With the above opening lines, the Book of the Acts of the Apostles reveals the identity of the emerging Easter Church. Without going into the specifics of its identity at this point, I can already speak to its manifestation in the "Faith Community" of my own experience at St. Pius X. The signs and wonders done among the people by the hands of the faithful and clergy are verifiable in the facts of a year and some months presented as follows:

1. At the beginning of 2015, Father Sean Carroll, SJ, from the Jesuit Kino Border Initiative at Nogales, Arizona on the Mexican border, shared the experiences of ministering to people seeking shelter and humane living with the St. Pius X

community. And the members of St. Pius X responded with whole-hearted generous support.

2. To light their Lenten path for 2015, Father Felix Just, SJ, from the Spiritual Center in Orange, California, opened for the members of St. Pius X, the words of Scripture and roused their hunger for the wisdom of God.

3. For the 2016 Lenten journey, Father Thomas Santa, with wit and humor, revealed the depth of mercy in the stories and parables of Jesus, and the people of St. Pius X responded with the ardor of spiritual longing.

4. At Easter 2015, the news of Kyla Mueller's murder at the hands of terrorists in Syria deeply touched people of goodwill around the world. She was on a humanitarian mission serving the poor and the needy in refugee camps. For us at St. Pius X, her death touched us in a special way because she was not only a missionary of mercy, but she was like one of us -- from Prescott, Arizona. As a sign of Spiritual oneness in grief, faith in God, hope in the resurrection,

and life giving-love, a Prayer Bouquet was sent to the Mueller family as an eternal memorial.

5.   Mid-year 2015 saw a string of death-and-illness-news that affected the clergy of St. Pius X. The death of Mr. Harry Ledwith, Sr., the Pastor's father, was followed by the hospitalization of both the Parochial Vicar and the Pastor. On February 24, 2016, the faith community of St. Pius X lost Fr. Bill Dougherty, CP, a great preacher of soul-searching sermons for many years. The community bonded together and reached out to their spiritual fathers, friends, and fellow disciples with an outpouring of grief, prayers and goodwill.

6. In 2015, the Habitat for Humanity Housing Project for those in need, which has become a supported tradition for the St. Pius X community, drew a robust fundraising response from the community and parishioners who helped with the actual building at two homes.

7. The 2015 Diocesan emerging media seminar hosted by St. Pius X, under the

watchful eagle's eye of the Director of Youth ministry, provided the community with a unique opportunity to gain new insights into the language of our technological age.

8. The Health Fair in October, 2015 hosted by the nurses and faculty of the University of Arizona, served the St. Pius X community with the promise of physical and psychological healing.

9. During the 2015 Thanksgiving season, St. Pius X community donated food for 181 families. Sixty more fabulous turkeys were sent to Cristo Rey orphanage in Nogales, Mexico, with a $500 donation. Turkeys were also sent to Casa Maria, the Catholic Worker House in Tucson, where each month, volunteers from the parish provide 600 lunches.

10. At the beginning of Advent 2015, from the faith community's Angel tree, over 500 children received quality gifts for Christmas.

11. On December 12, 2015, at the fundraising music extravaganza for the JUHRI project in Nigeria, St. Pius raised more than $11,500. The aim of the

Joseph Ukpo Hospitals and Research Institutes (JUHRI) is to bring health care to those most in need in the rural villages in Southern Nigeria.

Talk of signs and wonder! The spirit of the Risen Lord is alive and active. There are many more signs and wonders, also in our Christian Churches today, worthy of mention. St. Pius X is just one living example. The point being made from the above data is not so much about the high esteem that people have for St. Pius X faith community nor the number of new members that have joined the parish. And for the records, St. Pius has its multitude of adorers and others who have joined her ranks of disciples, especially at Easter Vigil ceremonies. Rather, the data reveals the unique identity of St. Pius X faith community as an "Easter Church" where *"Alleluia, the Lord is risen"* is their anthem.

Like the Easter Church of the Acts of the Apostles, St. Pius X has an inward spiritual life lived and fostered in communion. The members reach out to each other and to others, sharing their pains and sorrows, joys, and hopes. Like the Easter Church of the Acts of the Apostles, the Easter Alleluia Parish of St. Pius X is a Church with people like Peter, John, and the Emmaus-bound group. There are the hesitant like Thomas and loving hearts like Mary of Magdala and the hidden followers like Joseph of Arimathea and Nicodemus. These men and women often, daily defeated by human weaknesses and doubts, never give up in total despair. Instead, with a reserve of trust they encounter the Risen Lord individually and in community. The result is a transformed community to which, *"A large number of people from the towns ... gathered, bringing the sick and those disturbed by unclean spirits and they were all cured"*.

We are no different than the Easter Church of the Acts of the Apostles (Acts 5:15-16). We still, the grieving, the needy, the unloved, the sick, the rejects, and marginalized find healing, succor and our community, home. Recall the gospel narrative of the Lord's passion. The disciples, who had all fled on Good Friday, were in hiding on the Resurrection day fearing for the worst. They refused to listen to the gossips' of some women and rumors of the Resurrection from Peter and the beloved disciple. But there came the Risen Lord's breath-taking *"epiphany"* as it were. Wow! Wow! Wow! Faced with the Risen Lord, still with the marks of the wounds from the nails, there is pin-drop silence. Then there followed the soothing words addressed to drooping hearts from a merciful heart.

Jesus' first magic words were *"Shalom! Peace be with you!"* Intentionally and deliberately intoned to take away the veil of suspicion and make room for trust between Jesus and his fearful and confused disciples. The second uttering of *"Shalom"* did the magic. It mended the scattered community of the Apostles and restored the physical and psychological balance of its members (Jn. 20:19-31). It was peace unearned but gifted, to signal unconditional forgiveness from a heart that can only bestow unlimited mercy.

Now restored and vivified, the transformed disciples are sent on mission guided by the Holy Spirit to perform signs and wonders intended to forgive sins and mend communities, heal the sick, feed the hungry, give water to the thirsty, clothe the naked, visit those imprisoned, and revive drooping spirits.

"As the father has sent me so I send you" (Jn. 20:21). The code words for the instructions of Jesus to his disciples then and now, are Shalom and Merciful-forgiveness: *"Be at peace and give peace; forgive as you have been forgiven and be merciful as you have been looked upon with mercy."* The Gospel message of Easter resonates with the experiences of the faith community of St. Pius X, and we have witnessed to the testament of the compassionate deeds of its members.

In the Jubilee Year of Mercy, having accepted and embraced God's mandate of peace and merciful forgiveness, I ask the faith community of St. Pius X and other faith communities everywhere, how resolved are you, as Easter-Faith communities, to continue to help God's merciful forgiveness take flesh in more people and in more places beyond our communities? Peter, Thomas, and all the fragile and flawed members of the Easter Church of the Acts of the Apostles, could accomplish many signs and wonders because they kept faith in community. We all are the same simple and flawed people of God. How does our membership in our respective faith communities help us say with Thomas, *"My Lord and my God?"*

May the Lord accept us and our
supplication.
*Lord our God, we believe in the Risen
Lord!*
Even in our doubts as individuals
and as flawed faith communities,
by the power of the Holy Spirit
consecrate us in thy truth.
Send us on your mission of unconditional
forgiveness and mercy.
Amen.

Chapter Fourteen. The CWC of Mercy

On Easter Sunday, March 27, 2016, in the city of Lahore, Pakistan, militant Islamists massacred Christian families celebrating Easter, leaving 74 dead and 362 injured, 25 of them in critical conditions. About half the dead were children.[18] According to the Reuters and Trunews media reports, a member of the militant group that claimed responsibility for the massacre posted a message to the public that stated: "The target was Christians." Pope Francis and other world leaders condemned the massacre. Pope Francis, on Monday, March 28, 2016, in urging the Pakistani leaders to restore peace, especially, for religious minorities also said: *"Violence and murderous hatred lead only to pain and destruction; respect and fraternity are the only ways to achieve peace"* (Vatican Radio report).[19]

This Easter Sunday attack helps us put into perspective the Easter story of the Acts of the Apostles, especially, the witness of Peter and other believers (Acts 5:27-32, 40-41). Just as the hostility and intolerance existed in those who condemned and persecuted the early Church, so too, those extreme militants allow their hatred and misunderstanding of their Abrahamic faith, enshrined in their Holy Book, to persecute the followers of Jesus, whom they accept in the <u>Koran</u>, as a prophet.

In our time, with all persecuted people of faith, who even today, *"suffer dishonor for the sake of the name" (of Abraham's sons and daughters),"* we stand in solidarity. The challenge remains. In the Jubilee Year of Mercy, how can we condemn all forms of religious persecutions, human indignities, and threats to human freedom and at the same time, with our Church and Pope Francis, call the persecutors our brothers and sisters in God-in-Christ? The key is to draw inspiration from Peter and his companions. Peter told his fellow Jews the truth, *"You killed the author of life"* (Acts 3:15). But he tempered his accusation with wisdom adding, *"I know that you acted in ignorance"* (Acts 3:17). Like Peter we must courageously witness to religious tolerance, human dignity, and human freedom. But, we must do so in such a way that those who violate these values will be open to the voice of conscience that God has put in the hearts of all humankind.

The challenge for us is to think and behave differently, with: "The CWC of Mercy" as guide. The first C guides us to embrace a new Creed that draws its principles from the greatest sermon ever preached, The Sermon on the Mount (Mathew 5:1-3-12). Jesus taught and lived what he preached: *"Father forgive them"*. We too, must have it in our hearts to forgive those who violently persecute us and pray for them. *"Blessed are you when they insult you and persecute you ... because of me. Rejoice and be glad, for your reward will be great in heaven"* (Matthew 5:11-12a). Additionally, we must seek to share our forgiveness with others as children of God. That is our first C – Our Creed.

Our believing must lead us to worshiping *"the lamb that was slain"* and who is worthy to receive from us, *"honor, glory and blessing"* (Rev. 5:12). Thus from our earthly liturgical celebration, our Worship, we look forward to our eternal heavenly worship of *"the one who sits on the throne and of the Lamb"* (Rev. 5:13). In the Jubilee Year of Mercy, from our reverent liturgical self-presence before the throne of the triune God, we draw strength to witness to these things – religious tolerance, human dignity, and human freedom, under the guidance of the Holy Spirit. This is our W – Worship.

Our believing "in a merciful and forgiving" Jesus and adoring him "the Risen one," should lead us to being and becoming like him, the Risen Lord. In the gospel of John, not only does Jesus provide items for food (the big catch of fish), he also becomes the cook as well as the waiter, inviting his weary disciples to the table: *"Come, have breakfast."* (Jn. 21:12). He draws us to table, the embracing space, where differences of opinion and world views bow and melt away in deference to the needs of our common humanity, human nourishment. To be like Jesus, who fed all at his table of fraternity, respect, and love, challenges us and our Muslim brothers and sisters to a new vision, a physical and spiritual breakfast of mercy in our over-wearied world of destruction and hate. Our third C – is to behave like Jesus, the Risen Lord, with our Code of Behavior.

Our mission in the Jubilee Year of Mercy challenges us to question ourselves. How much do we know of the Abrahamic faith tradition that we share with believers of Judaism and Islam? How open are we to engage in inter-religious dialogue with followers of other religious traditions in order to share and witness publicly to our deepened faith in Jesus? If an opportunity for a joint public worship with other faith traditions presents itself this year, in our towns and cities, will you join others in order to witness to unity, fraternity, understanding and peace?

As believers in justice, human dignity and freedom will we, as a Church, join other religious groups to offer humanitarian services in war-torn places in order to witness to "The CWC of Mercy?" On Ecumenical dialogue, as the five hundredth anniversary of the Protestant reformation approaches in 2017, are we ready to join as the Body of Christ with our separated brothers and sisters, to pray the Lord's prayer for unity -- that we may be one (Jn. 17:20-21).

18. Website: https://thereligionofpeace.com/

19. Vatican Radio Report.

Chapter Fifteen. The Heralds of Mercy

Many years ago, our Seminary choir sang the exchange between Jesus and the Repentant Thief, on his right hand on the Cross, so movingly, that it turned into a frequent refrain for jokes in the seminary (Lk. 23:42-43). Whenever one was appointed the Prefect of the school or of the class, person in-charge of food or the refectory, Works master, or any post of responsibility, the student body would hum in unison the refrain: *"Remember us in your kingdom oh!"* Compared to the plea of the repentant thief, ours then was a plea for bending rules for self-indulgence.

The repentant thief's sentiment was more of an honest plea for divine restoration. *"Jesus remember me when you come into your kingdom!"* for him meant, *"Jesus, Joshua, Savior, Remember me, as I am in God, not as I am in my human mess."* And Jesus returned the compliment by reminding the repentant thief and us, of our original status as sons and daughters of God in God's World. Once a child of God, always a child of God -- there is no statute of limitation to who we are in God.

"Welcome home!" Jesus told the man born again on the Cross. Something tells me that it was an unimaginable moment for the man. Surprise beyond measure! Joy immeasurable, hope uncontemplated, merciful restoration gifted not merited, must be celebrated in some kind of break dance and song. To every generation of born-again men and women, the good thief recommends that his memorial, *"Remember Me"* be sung whenever the Gospel of his conversion is proclaimed: *Jesus-s, remember me-e! Jesus-s, remember me-e! Jesus-s, remember me, when you come into your Kingdom!*

Palm Sunday's reading, in good measure, is our divine homecoming and restoration as Jesus proclaims to our hearing, *"Today, you will be with me in paradise"*. But the question is: What has necessitated the restoration? Is it our failing to heed God's command to do good; to both ask for mercy when we need it and to give mercy when we can? What need we do now? The answer is in the Gospel. Just as Jesus turned to the repentant thief, he even now turns to us with a priceless offer – a room for us in his Kingdom. Today, in the Jubilee Year of Mercy, it is our turn to turn and look up to Jesus with transformed hearts of unconditional mercy on a mission of mercy to others.

In his Gospel, St. Luke narrates, at length, of Jesus forgiving "them." Anonymity here isn't intended. So who are the "them?" The "them" turns out to be both Jesus' enemies and friends. All are forgiven. The Jewish religious leaders, who accused him of blasphemy and demanded his execution, are forgiven. The soldiers, who nailed him mercilessly on the tree of the Cross, are forgiven. The Roman appointed administrator, Pontius Pilate, who gave in to the demands of the righteous, is forgiven. Peter, who denied him and the rest of the disciples who abandoned him, are forgiven (Lk. 22:14-23:56). All who didn't understand his message are forgiven!

The reason for Jesus' unconditional restoration of the repentant thief should now be very understandable. Though he did not explicitly demand forgiveness, his cry, *"Remember me"*

was an acknowledgement of who Jesus was --
a merciful God. Therefore, just as Jesus
forgives 'them' all, he forgives those of us who
have more often than not behaved like the
"them" who mess up our lives, not knowing
what we do.

Every Palm Sunday, Jesus invites us to be "Co-
Heralds of Mercy!" The palms blessed, are
symbols of our ongoing divine/human
homecoming and restoration. With them in
our hands, we proclaim Jesus' unconditional
mercy and forgiveness towards all.

And now, our challenge remains – to be
heralds of divine mercy to others. Which
brother or sister, which man or woman,
which cleaned-up addict or former
prisoner do you remember? Are you
ready to be the first to look at them with
mercy, welcome and forgive them from
the heart?

JESUS, RECUERDAME! JESUS
RECUERDAME! JESUS
RECUERDAME CUANDO LLEGUES A
TU REINO!

Chapter Sixteen. The Uhuru of Mercy

In the "Today" news of January 15, 2016, Jordi Lippe-McGraw reported the moving reunion of a 6-year old boy, Kane, with his pet dog, Kase, who had been missing for a month. According to Jordi's report, the month before, Paula Williams, Kane's mother, in company with her son, let Kase outside to relieve himself. When they went to bring him back inside, they discovered that he was gone. Kane cried his heart out as they could not find Kase.

Weeks after Kase went missing, Paula was driving home, when suddenly she saw a dog running up to two school girls alighting from the school bus. She pulled over and said, "That's my son's dog!" The family of the two girls said, in their defense, that the dog had come to their house almost a month ago. In the snow and freezing weather, they took him in and gave him a warm place to stay. Paula was grateful to the family of the two girls and could hardly wait to take Kase to reunite with his grieving young owner, Kane.

On being reunited with his dog, the overjoyed Kane said to Kase, "I missed you!" as he bear-hugged his furry friend. The dog, in response, tongue-splashed Kane's face licking him passionately. Kase, having survived the stress/distress of separation and having been reunited with his owner, seemed to be saying, like the multitude in the book of Revelation, standing *"before the throne and the lamb ... wearing white robes and holding palms branches,"UHURH!*[20] Like Kase and the multitude, the Book of Revelation gives us and disciples of all generations who *"have survived the time of great distress"* and *"washed their robes and made them white in the blood of the lamb,"* a pledge of UHURU -Protection, Security, Safety and Salvation (Rev. 7:9, 14-17). Why? Because, like Kase who has Kane, we believers have the Good Shepherd (Jn. 10:27-30).

We listen, hear, and follow Jesus, our Good Shepherd, not blindly, but because, through him, we hear the Father's voice. Like the lost Kase, we are the open-hearted who see, hear and recognize our Good Shepherd. Like Kase, we are *Anawim,* the poor of the Lord, who trust and hope in our Good Shepherd because our hearts are not closed. No one can snatch us from him because we have been entrusted to him by God our Father. The emphasis here is on what Jesus does, namely, shepherding us. He is the one that John in Revelation pledges will *"wipe away every tear from {our] eyes;* *"and lead [us] to springs of living water."*

In the Jubilee Year of Mercy, *"The Uhuru of Mercy"* is the Shepherd's pledge that our daily struggles will one day be over, our wounds and injuries will be healed and our tears will be wiped away. We will have a home and shelter in our shepherd's heart. No opposition to our faith in the Risen Lord will succeed. Our century, like the time of the Acts of the Apostles, is a time of stress and distress, opposition time, injury, wounded time and a time of grinding daily struggles. Ours is a time, like no other, when swords and persecutions want to have the last word on human dignity, human freedom, freedom of expression, and freedom of religion. Ours is a time that could seriously lead believers to compromise their faith.

But we have some lessons to learn from the Apostles. Like Paul and Barnabas in the face of opposition and persecution and because of our faith in Christ, we are challenged to seek other creative ways of witnessing rather than despair or seeking revenge. Like the Apostles, we too must re-configure our attitudes and become *"a light ... an instrument of salvation to the ends of the earth."* To do this with joy, like the Apostles, we must seek the guidance the Holy Spirit, whom, Jesus told us, he left with us for that purpose. (Luke 24:49)

Lately we have seen all over television, newspapers, videos, iPhones and internets, how Christians, minority groups, and others are blatantly persecuted around the world. On Good Shepherd Sunday, Jesus, the Good Shepherd has invited us to join him, even now, in the process of healing and drying the tears of the wounded and persecuted. Like the Apostles, we are challenged to proactive, creative witnessing. How do we do that? First, we need to pray for those persecuted for their religious beliefs. Second, join proactive groups, like the Knights of Columbus or other organizations of goodwill, to tell the truth about the genocide against Christians and other religious minorities in the Middle East and beyond. Third, there are so many former members of countless parishes who have been hurt and angered by the Church. For these and other reasons, they have been separated from their faith community and practices of the faith.

Will you invite one or more of such people to the "homecoming" experiences at: Faith Interrupted RCIA, Cursillo and Marriage Encounter programs in many parishes? And finally, like Paula and Kane who kept searching for their dog until they found him, how can we become co-shepherds with the Risen Lord to search, find and carry home the needy with warmth, security and love?

Oh God,
open wide our ears!
Challenge us to hear
"The Uhuru of Mercy" of the Good
Shepherd
in unexpected creatures, places, peoples
and cultures.
Help us shake off our fears.

With renewed courage and mercy
may we embrace the truth of a wider
inclusiveness
to give protection, security, safety and
peace to all!
Amen.

20. *Uhuru* is a word heard very often in East Africa generally accepted to mean "Freedom." Interestingly, the name of the sitting President of Kenya is Uhuru Kenyatta.

Chapter Seventeen. The Present and Future of Mercy

After the Captain of the Eagle, Apollo 11 lunar module guided the craft to a safe landing on the Moon at 4:17 pm EDT, July 20, 1969, his first words were: *"Houston, Tranquility Base here. The Eagle has landed."* Thereafter, Neil Armstrong, as he stepped out of Eagle onto the Moon, said, *"That's a small step for a man, one giant leap for mankind."* In a "60 Minute" interview in 2005 he recalled what he saw on the moon after that *"small step"* moment: *"The horizon seems quite close to you because the curvature is so much more pronounced than on earth."*[21]

Years later, Buzz Aldrin recalled their moments together on the moon, *"Whenever I look at the Moon I am reminded of that precious moment ... when Neil and I stood on the desolate, barren, yet beautiful Sea of Tranquility, looking back at our brilliant blue Earth suspended in the darkness of space. I realized that even though we were farther away from Earth than two humans had ever been we were not alone. The entire world took the journey with us.*[22]*"* With one *"small step,"* Neil Armstrong and his crew brought the present and the future together and opened for mankind a vision of "a new heaven and a new earth" not unlike the "new heaven and the new earth" of the Book of Revelation (Rev. 21:1-5).

The only difference between Armstrong's "new heaven and new earth" and that of the Book of Revelation is that while that new heaven and earth of Revelation will come when God decides, Armstrong's is happening right now and is ongoing. The hope of us living in space, at some point in time, is no more a pipe dream; even now people have started living and working up there at the space station. With this comparison, I am reminding us of the incredible self-sacrifice by Neil Armstrong and his crew, for us.

What we might enjoy in the future is happening even now. But this all happened because of one man's "small step." In line with Armstrong's "small step" of already celebrating the new heaven and a new earth, we disciples of Christ should also, even now, begin to celebrate the heavenly Jerusalem by our individual and communal "small steps" of gospel love as commanded by the Risen Lord.

How should we celebrate the Lord's command of loving one another in the Jubilee Year of Mercy? The attitude and the actions of the astronauts provide us with examples to emulate.

In this Jubilee Year of Mercy we have lessons to learn from the Astronauts to inspire us on our mission of mercy. Just as the self-sacrifice of Neil Armstrong, Mike Collins and Buzz Aldrin of Apollo 11 and many other Astronauts since then, have inspired the world to long for life in space, our love for the heavenly Jerusalem should inspire us to concretely embrace compassionate, self-sacrificing deeds for others in our world "where God-in-Christ dwells with our human race." Even as God will dwell with us his people then in the heavenly Jerusalem, he dwells with his people today in our loving deeds to others. God is the only one who will in the end, *adequately "wipe away every tear... banish death, mourning, wailing and pain "*.

But, we can, even now, begin the process of bringing about the bliss of the heavenly Jerusalem. In doing this we should adopt the attitude of Apostles, especially, Paul and

Barnabas. In spite of the incitement, jealousy, persecution and violent abuse and eventual expulsion from Antioch, they never despaired or sought revenge (Acts 13:14, 43-52). Rather, with deep faith in the Risen Lord, they became creative in seeking other ways to evangelize the people. With the command of the Lord to *"love one another,"* as their secret weapon, they turned the world of their time upside down. With grace-filled attitude and the good news, they worked wonders and strengthened the spirits of the disciples (Acts 14:21-27).

As was the case with the Apostles so also is it with us, *"all will know that [we] are [Christ's] disciples if we have love for one another [and for others]"* (Jn. 13-31-35). Like Neil Armstrong and other astronauts, with little "small steps" of self-sacrifice today, our eagle will land at God's tranquility base in readiness for the full celebration of our new heaven and new earth according to God's will and time.

Lord of merciful love
keep us mindful that, even now,
that the present and the future
of Mercy for mankind

depends on our "small steps" of self-
sacrifice for others.
With our individual and communal
"small steps" of self-sacrifice,
send us forth on mission to all the people
we will meet today,
around us and beyond us.
Through the Holy Spirit, working in and
through us,
may we, by our compassionate deeds,
inaugurate the joys of the "new heaven
and the new earth."
With the enabling inner joy of the Holy
Spirit
may we overcome every temptation
with gospel love!
Amen.

21. https:enwikiquoteorg/wiki/Neil_Armstrong

22. Buzz Aldrin, remembered in Neil Armstrong's "True American Hero and the Best Pilot I ever knew", Huffington Post – August, 2005.

The Creed of Mercy - The Beatitudes (Mt. 5:3-12a)

Blessed are the poor in Spirit,

- o For theirs is the kingdom of heaven.

Blessed are they who mourn,

- o For they shall be comforted.

Blessed are the meek,

- o For they will inherit the land.

Blessed are they who hunger and thirst for righteousness,

- o For they will be satisfied.

Blessed are the merciful,

- o For they shall obtain mercy.

Blessed are the clean of heart,

- o For they will see God.

Blessed are the peacemakers,

- o For they will be called children of God.

Blessed are they who are persecuted for the sake of righteousness,

- o For theirs is the kingdom of heaven.

Blessed are you when they insult you and persecute you and utter every kind of evil against you [falsely] because of me,

- o Rejoice and be glad, for your reward will be great in heaven

About the Author

Monsignor Michael Otto Ekpenyong is a priest of the Catholic Diocese of Uyo, Nigeria. He has an MA in Philosophy and a Ph.D. in Systematic Theology from Duquesne University, Pittsburgh, Pennsylvania.

Ordained thirty-nine years ago, Monsignor Ekpenyong is on Sabbatical in the Diocese of Tucson, Arizona. He has served in the parishes of St. Anthony of Padua, Casa Grande and St. Rose of Lima, Safford. Presently he is the Parochial Vicar at St. Pius X Parish, Tucson.

In <u>Flickers of Mercy</u>, Msgr. Michael Ekpenyong provides us with mercy moments from his rich experience both at home in Nigeria, in other African nations as well as his recent service at St Pius X Parish, in the Sonoran Desert, in the Diocese of Tucson" Most Rev. Gerald F. Kicanas, D.D., Bishop of Tucson.

"Go with your heart in dealing with your own humankind.

Then you will walk by faith in merciful love and not by sight"

from "The Appearances of Mercy" – Msgr. Michael Ekpenyong

Made in the USA
Charleston, SC
25 June 2016